RECLAIMING
the SPIRITUALS

RECLAIMING the SPIRITUALS

New Possibilities for African American Christian Education

YOLANDA Y. SMITH

WIPF & STOCK · Eugene, Oregon

*In love and appreciation to my parents,
Louis and Vera Smith,
who inspired me to sing, to dance,
and to embrace my dreams*

Wipf and Stock Publishers
199 W 8th Ave, Suite 3
Eugene, OR 97401

Reclaiming the Spirituals
New Possibilities for African American Christian Education
By Smith, Yolanda Y.
Copyright©2004 Pilgrim Press
ISBN 13: 978-1-60899-591-2
Publication date 7/26/2010
Previously published by Pilgrim Press, 2004

This limited edition licensed by special permission of The Pilgrim Press.

Contents

Preface ... vii

Introduction: Roll, Jordan, Roll ... 1
    Teaching through the Spirituals: New Possibilities / 1
    The Triple-Heritage and the Spirituals / 3

1. Ain't Dat Good News? Teaching the Triple-Heritage through the African American Spirituals ... 9
    Defining a Triple-Heritage Model of Christian Education / 12

2. Deep River: Exploring the Triple-Heritage ... 21
    A Holistic View / 21
    Components of the Triple-Heritage / 22
    Implications for Christian Education in the African American Church / 47

3. I'm Gonna Sing: Exploring the Spirituals ... 55
    Nature of the Spirituals / 55
    Characteristics / 58
    Historical Background / 62
    The Spirituals as a Source for Enhancing the Educational Ministry in the African American Church / 77

4. This Little Light of Mine: Theology and Christian Education in the African American Church ... 83
    Black Theology, Womanist Theology, and Christian Education / 83
    Insights from Black Theology and Womanist Theology for a Triple-Heritage Model of Christian Education / 95

5. **Balm in Gilead: The Theology of the Spirituals**   102

    God / 102
    Jesus / 103
    Holy Spirit / 104
    Humanity / 106
    Sin and Evil / 108
    Eschatology / 109
    Christian Ethics / 111
    Insights from the Spirituals for a Triple-Heritage Model of Christian Education / 111

6. **Let Us Break Bread Together: Using the Spirituals to Teach the Triple-Heritage**   116

    Dialogue / 116
    Imagination / 120
    Spontaneity / 122
    Rhythm / 126
    Narrative / 130
    Nature / 132
    Ritual / 136

7. **My Soul's Been Anchored in de Lord: Insights for Building a Triple-Heritage Model of Christian Education**   144

    Pastoral Leadership / 144
    Teacher Training / 145
    Nurture / 146
    Creative Methodology / 147
    Creative Programming / 148
    Curriculum Resources / 149
    Fun / 150
    Reclaiming the Spirituals / 152

Publication Acknowledgments   155

Bibliography   159

Index   173

Preface

As a black woman, I have long had an interest in Christian education from an African American perspective. It is an interest initially rooted in a variety of experiences that I have had (good and bad) in the public school system and through my involvement in Sunday school as well as in other Christian education programs within the church. Most of my secular education has been in predominantly Anglo schools. In the early years of my life, I found that the public school system was able to provide me with basic academic skills, but it was not able to address my cultural needs. African Americans as well as many other minorities were either left out of the curriculum altogether, or they were portrayed negatively whenever they were included. I always came away from this experience struggling to create a positive self-image as well as an appreciation for my heritage.

Throughout my childhood, my family attended Anglo churches. Although it was at one of these churches, at the age of seventeen, that I eventually experienced a spiritual conversion and made a commitment to God, this experience was not enough to address my identity crisis or to instill in me a sense of pride and appreciation for my heritage.

When I entered college, I began to attend an African American church and, for the first time, I felt that I was at home. I felt like I belonged, and I knew that I had finally found the source of my true identity. In this church, I saw African American women and men who were successful role models, who were prominent figures in the community, and who had a great sense of pride in their culture.

During my early years at this church, I had a deep desire to learn more about God, especially in light of my African American heritage. I found, however, the overall educational ministry of the church, like others that I had attended, to be inadequate to address this need.

For instance, there was usually only one teaching method used in the classes: the lecture method. The majority of the class time was spent either listening to the lecture or reading through the Sunday school book without sufficient time for exploration or reflection on the biblical text. Although the lack of variety of teaching methods and techniques is not peculiar to African American churches, it was especially disturbing to me as an African American because many of the rich resources of the African American oral tradition, such as music, dance, poetry, ritual, proverbs, metaphors, stories, and historical accounts, had been replaced by print resources that were primarily developed by white denominations. More importantly, there was often a heavy emphasis on Christian doctrine without much attention to our heritage. Although the heritage was often celebrated during worship and through a variety of activities on special days, it was not usually emphasized in the educational ministry or its curriculum. Moreover, while there was a concern for personal and spiritual application, there was little emphasis, in the educational ministry, on social application within the community. Rather, the social emphasis was more readily observed during worship and other church events.

As I began to prepare for a career in Christian education, I continued to ponder this dilemma. However, in the course of my studies and deeper involvement in the life of the church and community, it became apparent that African American Christians have a unique "triple-heritage" that encompasses their African, African American, and Christian roots.[1] I was particularly impressed by the realization that the triple-heritage could be a viable resource for Christian education. Naturally arising out of the African American experience and its traditions, this heritage embodies a rich variety of sources. It draws upon the diverse cultural traditions of the African motherland, including tribal customs, naming ceremonies, rituals, music, dance, literature, and kinship patterns. It also draws upon the African American legacy of sheroes and heroes who have literally built this country upon their backs. And finally, it draws upon the myriad rituals and customs formed by the African American encounter with Christianity.

Unfortunately, contemporary Christian education for African Americans has failed to fully acknowledge and embrace the triple-heritage and its implications for Christian education, the church, and the wider community. Most often, the educational ministries of many African American churches do not fully reflect the full scope of the triple-heritage. For example, Christian doctrines or African American history is often emphasized with little or no attention to African religious or cultural roots. Consequently, African Americans are in danger of losing valuable aspects of their heritage and its educational and prophetic influence. The late Grant Shockley, formerly professor of Christian Education at Duke Divinity School, and Ella Mitchell, an African American religious scholar, professor, and preacher, also shared the concern that many African American churches have adopted models of Christian education that do not reflect their heritage.[2] Although black churches prior to the Civil War incorporated indigenous modes of preaching, ritualizing, singing, and praying, Mitchell notes that in the area of education, many churches patterned themselves after white educational programs to provide a "more 'proper' religious instruction than had been provided, presumably, by the oral tradition."[3] This trend, unfortunately, appears to continue in many African American churches even today. Thus, it is essential that African American Christians find new ways of experiencing, expressing, and teaching their faith and culture. One way to do so is by developing vibrant models of Christian education that emphasize their triple-heritage.

This book attempts to encourage and aid contemporary African American churches in reclaiming their full heritage as Africans, African Americans, and Christians. It encourages African Americans to draw upon the wisdom of their rich cultural and spiritual heritage as a viable and relevant resource for the development of a model of Christian education that will empower African American Christians as they face the challenges of the twenty-first century. While integrating the three distinctive components of the triple-heritage, this model of African American Christian education emphasizes and illuminates the central role of the spirituals. However, the spirituals not only serve as a key component of a new model of African American Christian education, but their use will also suggest how the triple-heritage can be appropriated as a broader resource for multicultural approaches to contemporary Christian education. My hope in writing this book is to provide a resource for religious educators in both the church and the academy to explore African American Christian heritage as well as to engage in a broader dialogue across diverse cultures and traditions.

I am grateful to a host of people who have journeyed with me throughout this process. I first began to explore the ideas for this project as a doctoral student at Claremont School of Theology in Claremont, California. I would like to express my sincere appreciation to Mary Elizabeth Moore, Karen Baker-Fletcher, Michele Foster, Frank Rogers, and Cornish Rogers for the countless hours they invested in my work as well as my personal and academic development. I also want to thank Elaine Walker, Linden Youngquist, Sarah Alexander, Sheila Marchbanks, Venus Butler, Linda Hickmon-Evans, and Jeff Brockman for their endless prayers, enduring friendship, and editorial assistance. In addition, I want to thank Kaudie McLean and Pamela Johnson for their editorial guidance and support.

I am grateful to the students in my Christian religious education courses, who were willing to explore new ideas and to envision new possibilities for the practice and theory of Christian religious education. I am especially thankful for those students who participated in my "Christian Education in the African American Experience" courses at both Iliff School of Theology and Yale Divinity School, where the ideas for this model of Christian education were more readily explored. In addition, I extend a special thank-you to the Pan African Women's Fellowship and the Black Seminarians at Yale Divinity School for their continuous prayers and support.

I also extend my sincere appreciation to my colleagues Margaret Farley, Letty Russell, Shannon Clarkson, Kristen Leslie, Serene Jones, David Bartlett, Moses Moore, Rebecca Chopp, Anne Wimberly, James Cone, Joseph Crockett, and James Evans for offering advice, encouragement, and valuable feedback on my work at various stages of development.

Special thanks to Pastor Warren H. Stewart Sr. and the First Institutional Baptist Church family, who have inspired my ministry, instilled a passion for the triple-heritage, and taught me to be faithful and to trust in God. I will always be grateful for their prayers, financial support, and encouragement. I also want to thank Pastor James Carrington and the Friendship Baptist Church family for embracing me during my tenure at Claremont. Their financial support and encouragement over those years has been greatly appreciated.

I want to thank the American Baptist Churches, USA; the Fund for Theological Education; Claremont School of Theology; and the Wabash Center for Teaching and Learning for providing financial assistance during my studies and subsequent writing of this book.

Last, but certainly not least, I want to thank my family, Louis and Vera Smith, parents; Angela Smith, sister; Valencia and Maceo Ward, sister and brother-in-law; April Black, niece; Maceo Jr., Michael, and Matthew Ward, nephews; and Alijah Black, great-nephew. I am deeply grateful for their love, commitment to family, and the many sacrifices that they have made on my behalf. They have always believed in me and encouraged me to reach for my dreams. For this, I am eternally grateful. I love you all, and I thank God for the precious gift of family.

Notes

1. Dr. Warren H. Stewart Sr. used the term "triple-heritage" to introduce his vision for an African American Christian Training School (AACTS), which he later established at the First Institutional Baptist Church of Phoenix, Arizona. AACTS is a Saturday school that provides a special program of study through the church, for children in kindergarten through tenth grade. The school has been in operation for approximately twelve years and has a curriculum that emphasizes African, American, and Christian resources.

2. Grant S. Shockley, "Christian Education and the Black Church," in *Christian Education Journey of Black Americans: Past, Present, Future,* compiled by Charles Foster, Ethel R. Johnson, and Grant S. Shockley (Nashville: Discipleship Resources, 1985), 14; Ella Mitchell, "Oral Tradition: Legacy of Faith for the Black Church," *Religious Education* 81, no. 1 (Winter 1986): 106, 109–11.

3. Ella Mitchell, "Oral Tradition," 106.

Introduction

Roll, Jordan, Roll

To go back to tradition is the first step forward.
—African proverb

Christian education from an African American perspective can help African Americans embrace their full heritage through a holistic curriculum that incorporates *all* three aspects of the triple-heritage. Teaching the triple-heritage challenges the African American church to embrace its African heritage, encouraging African Americans to reclaim African history, culture, and geography as their ancestral heritage; its African American heritage, illuminating the experience and significant contributions of African Americans in the United States; and its Christian heritage, affirming the fullness of Christian experience and the distinctiveness of African American Christianity. By teaching the triple-heritage, African Americans can preserve and celebrate both their faith and their cultural heritage.

My desire is to explore creative ways that the church can be involved in teaching the triple-heritage of African Americans. Teaching the triple-heritage in a positive light can lead to a sense of pride in African American heritage and allow persons of the African Diaspora to live with confidence, self-respect, dignity, and freedom in society.

Teaching through the Spirituals: New Possibilities

One way to teach the triple-heritage creatively is by reclaiming the African American spirituals. Since all three aspects of the triple-heritage have informed the spirituals, the spirituals can be used to explore the three streams of the triple-heritage. For example, African traditional music has influenced the rhythm, worldview, and spontaneous nature of the spirituals. The African American experience of slavery gave birth to the spirituals through the secret religious meetings, the work environment, and the harsh realities of bondage. And Christianity has inspired numerous theological themes in these songs, revealing the faith of a people who have endured great hardships and oppression. The spirituals, therefore, form a point of intersection where the three components of the triple-heritage come together and where reflection on the triple-heritage can begin.[1] A striking example is the spiritual "Steal Away." In it, the African component is seen in the hidden embedded meaning.

> Steal away, steal away, steal away to Jesus!
> Steal away, steal away home,
> I ain't got long to stay here!

Incorporating hidden or coded meanings in music is a common African practice designed to obscure the true meaning of a particular message or to critique certain situations. Thus, slaves incorporated a long-standing African custom when they used "Steal Away" as a signal for secret meetings or religious gatherings.[2] An examination of this spiritual and others may shed light on various African customs and practices and their carryovers in slave communities.

Likewise, "Steal Away" has an African American component in that it reflects the slaves' quest for survival and liberation.

> My Lord calls me, He calls me by the thunder;
> The trumpet sounds with-in-a my soul,
> I ain't got long to stay here.

This verse could have been a signal for an impending escape, as the words "I ain't got long to stay here" seem to imply. They thus point us to some of the creative ways that the slaves resisted slavery, the Underground Railroad led by Harriet Tubman being but one of the examples of successful efforts by slaves to free themselves. In her efforts to guide the slaves to freedom, Tubman reportedly incorporated numerous spirituals, including "Steal Away."[3] In a similar fashion, "Steal Away" played a significant role in Nat Turner's insurrection, so much so that some have considered him to be the most likely author of this song.[4]

Moreover, "Steal Away" reflects the Christian component by revealing the slaves' understanding of God. They saw Jesus as friend and liberator and believed that God would one day deliver them from the bonds of slavery.

> My Lord calls me, He calls me by the lightning,
> The trumpet sounds with-in-a my soul,
> I ain't got long to stay here.

By exploring the spirituals, then, African Americans can gain insight into their African roots, their African American history, and their Christian faith.[5]

The Triple-Heritage and the Spirituals

My goal is not to make a sharp distinction among the three aspects of the triple-heritage; rather, my intention is to show that they are closely related and that they are intimately intertwined. The triple-heritage is a unit with three vital components that together make up a unique whole. There is a dynamic relationship among the three elements: They draw upon one another, they flow out of each other, and they build upon each other.

A metaphor that seems to capture the essence of the triple-heritage is that of three rivers.[6] Each river has its own place of origin and its own distinct characteristics. When they flow together, however, they create a new body of water, and the distinctive characteristics of each can no longer be completely separated. For example, the African survivals that are still present today are not easily identified as African traditions or practices. Because they have been so immersed in the African American culture, sharp distinctions between the African elements and other African American traditions and practices are often difficult to discern.

Each aspect of the triple-heritage contributes something valuable and distinctive to the African American Christian heritage, and together they make up the whole heritage. While one aspect may be more dominant than the others, all three contribute uniquely to the

Introduction

whole. All three of the original streams have also continued to flow in distinctive directions, as in the multitude of African, African American, and Christian traditions; thus, distinctive streams continue to enrich the lives of African American Christian people.

While numerous resources could inform a curriculum that centers on the triple-heritage of African Americans, I have chosen to focus on the African American spirituals for several reasons. First, as noted above, the spirituals actually embody the triple-heritage. They are not only grounded in African traditions, but they were also born out of the American experience of slavery and significantly shaped by Christian doctrine.[7]

Second, I am interested in exploring the spirituals because they easily lend themselves to critical analysis of the culture and reflection upon personal and collective responsibility within the community. Indeed, since their inception, the spirituals have been used as a form of social critique. This critique can be seen in numerous songs that embody a spirit of protest and a challenge to bring about transformation and social change.

Third, the spirituals can enhance the educational ministry of the African American church by providing a means for exploring the triple-heritage in a way that allows all three aspects of the triple-heritage to be reflected fully in relation to each other. A full representation is essential so that one aspect of the heritage does not dominate the curriculum while other aspects are lost. The aim is to see the triple-heritage as a whole, with interrelated components, rather than as three separate and distinct elements.

Fourth, by drawing upon the theology embodied in the spirituals, the church can reflect upon the movement of the Holy Spirit in the life of the African American church. This reflection sheds light on how the church has been empowered by the Holy Spirit and inspired with a sense of hope for the future. This hope has allowed African Americans to envision freedom from oppression. The movement of the Holy Spirit through music and song united the enslaved community, provided comfort in the midst of hardship, and deepened the church's sense of spirituality.[8] A similar awareness of the movement of the Holy Spirit is needed in the church today. The church must continue to have a sense of hope, a commitment to fight injustice and oppression, and a passion for deepening its relationship with God. These elements come through the inspiration and power of the Holy Spirit.

Moreover, the spirituals can aid the church in moving towards a "Spirit-centered" education,[9] for the Spirit of God empowers the church as well as individuals to carry out the mission and ministry of Jesus Christ. This ministry reflects God's love, hope, peace, justice, healing, and wholeness. The Holy Spirit is vital to the educational ministry of the church because an effective Christian education ministry must depend upon the guidance and inspiration of the Holy Spirit; thus, Christian education ought to be Spirit-centered education. Christian education begins with the Spirit of God and works in harmony with the Spirit to meet the needs of the church and community.

Finally, on a more personal note, I am drawn to the spirituals because they have inspired me in profound ways: They have enhanced my spiritual growth by giving me a greater sense of the presence of God in my life and inspiring me to deepen my relationship with God; they have given me a sense of connection with, as well as a profound respect for, my ancestors; they have allowed me to experience a fuller sense of community within the African American church; and they have helped me to gain a sense of pride in my African American heritage.

Unfortunately, many contemporary African American churches have adopted models of Christian education that have served to distance their congregations and ministries from the spirituals and other components of their triple-heritage. Having uncritically incorporated Eurocentric educational paradigms, curriculum resources, and modes of worship, African Americans have lost valuable aspects of their African, African American, and Christian heritage. As corrective, this book introduces a new approach and model of Christian education that is both grounded in and informed by the triple-heritage — African, African American, and Christian traditions that have historically shaped and given substance to the distinct religious, cultural, and spiritual experiences of African American Christians.

This book begins by exploring the triple-heritage model. The basic components of this model are introduced in chapter 1. Chapter 2 provides an introduction to each aspect of the triple-heritage: African,

African American, and Christian. The task of chapter 3 is to discuss the spirituals as embodiments of the triple-heritage by defining them, identifying their sources, and surveying their history, impact, and function. Chapter 4 explores the relationship between black theology, womanist theology, and Christian education, with particular attention to the theological insights for a triple-heritage model of Christian education. The theology of the spirituals and its implications for a triple-heritage model of Christian education is examined in chapter 5. Chapter 6 explores practical suggestions for how the spirituals can be used to teach the triple-heritage. Chapter 7 offers insights for building a triple-heritage model of Christian education.

As we embark upon the twenty-first century, the African American church must continue to explore new models of Christian education that will affirm and celebrate the uniqueness of the African American experience, nurture the Christian faith, develop quality educational programs, and promote social action within and beyond the African American community. Christian education that embraces the triple-heritage is just such a model. It holds true to the African proverb, "To go back to tradition is the first step forward." As African Americans build upon the wisdom of African and African American ancestors, they will be able to explore greater possibilities for Christian education in the African American church.

Notes

1. See chapter 1 for a full discussion and diagram of how the triple-heritage comes together in the spirituals.
2. Wyatt Tee Walker, *"Somebody's Calling My Name": Black Sacred Music and Social Change* (1979; reprint, Valley Forge, Pa.: Judson Press, 1990), 56, 58–59; Lawrence W. Levine, *Black Culture and Black Consciousness: Afro-American Folk Thought from Slavery to Freedom* (New York: Oxford University Press, 1977), 7–10; John Lovell Jr., *Black Song: The Forge and the Flame* (New York: Macmillan, 1972), 7–8, 40, 42, 45–46, 379; Miles Mark Fisher, *Negro Slave Songs in the United States* (1953; reprint, New York: Carol Publishing Group, 1981), 66–67; James H. Cone, *The Spirituals and the Blues* (1972; reprint, Maryknoll, N.Y.: Orbis Books, 1991), 15–16; William B. McClain, *Come Sunday: The Liturgy of Zion* (Nashville: Abingdon Press, 1990), 110–11; Harold A. Jackson Jr., "The

Negro Spiritual as Religious Expression and Historical Experience," *Journal of the Blaisdell Institute* 9, no. 1 (Fall and Winter 1973–74): 42–43; Harold A. Jackson Jr., "The New Hermeneutic and the Understanding of Spirituals," *Journal of the Interdenominational Theological Center* 33, no. 2 (Spring 1976): 44–45.

3. Lovell, 125, 379. For additional information on Harriet Tubman, see Sarah Bradford, *Harriet Tubman: The Moses of Her People* (Secaucus, N.J.: Citadel Press, 1961); M. W. Taylor, *Harriet Tubman* (New York: Chelsea House, 1991).

4. Lovell, 196; Wyatt Walker, 58–59; Fisher, 66–67; Harold Jackson, "New Hermeneutic," 45; Harold Jackson, "Negro Spiritual as Religious Expression," 42. See also Cone, *Spirituals and the Blues,* 16.

5. See chapters 3, 5, and 6 for a broader discussion of the spirituals as a source for exploring the triple-heritage.

6. This metaphor emerged out of a brainstorming session with Mary Elizabeth Moore, who offered several metaphors that might help to clarify the relationship among the three aspects of the triple-heritage.

7. Maud Cuney Hare, "The Source," in *The Negro in Music and Art,* ed. Lindsay Patterson, International Library of Negro Life and History (1935; reprint, New York: Publishers Company, 1967), 21–22.

8. Melva Wilson Costen, *African American Christian Worship* (Nashville: Abingdon Press, 1993), 44–47.

9. Frank Rogers, "Dancing with Grace: Toward a Spirit-Centered Education," *School of Theology at Claremont, Occasional Paper* 1, no. 2 (1991): 5.

One

Ain't Dat Good News?

Teaching the Triple-Heritage through the African American Spirituals

---

Several years ago, I had the privilege of visiting a Christian school in Los Angeles on a field assignment for my class in contemporary theories in religious education. Each student enrolled in the class was required to visit a religious education program that reflected a particular cultural perspective. Because my interest was in Christian education from an African American perspective, I selected a Christian school that was designed to meet the needs of African American children in the inner city. I was looking for good news.

During my brief visit, I observed the chapel service, a variety of classes, and the campus. I also interviewed the principal, students, and instructors, using questions I developed prior to the visit along with ones that emerged spontaneously.

The school impressed me in several ways. By 1993, it had become a fully accredited inner-city school, organized and sponsored by an African American church as part of its ministry. Founded twenty-three years previously with only 1 student and 1 teacher, the school had grown to an approximate enrollment of 450 students (325 families) and 20 African American teachers. The students were quiet and attentive in chapel as well as in the classroom. They played cooperatively with one another on the playground. The students listened to the lectures, followed the instructions for each lesson, and raised their hands to respond to questions. They allowed other students to speak without interruption and waited for their turn to respond. Teachers then praised the children for good work and good behavior. Additionally, the school's philosophy of education reflected the

Ain't Dat Good News?

school's commitment to "the principle of Academic Excellence, in an unashamedly Christian environment."[1] The principal noted that the aim of the school was to maintain a cooperative and supportive relationship with parents, teachers, and students. For instance, parents were expected to review and sign their child's homework every night. They were also encouraged to consult with the principal and teachers regarding any concerns. Furthermore, students were encouraged to interact with the principal and teachers as needed.

While I was impressed in many ways, I was also surprised to find that the classroom pictures portrayed biblical characters as white and the school used a Eurocentric approach to the Scriptures as well as to the overall classroom procedures. For example, the children were given Bible verses to learn by rote, to be recited individually to the class. In contrast, African-centered pedagogy stresses group learning, whereby requirements are mastered together. Children begin and complete a task together while supporting one another throughout the process.[2] Yet, from what I observed, these educational practices were not in use. Furthermore, no mention was made of the black presence in the Bible. What a disappointment! How could this happen in a predominantly African American school that claimed to embrace as well as promote African American heritage?

Given that this African American school was sponsored by an African American church, with mostly African American students and teachers, I expected to see the explicit reflection of the black experience in teaching methods, classroom procedures, and visual aids. Overall, this was not the case. Various components of the school reflected implicitly the African American experience, as in the case of references by one or two of the teachers to black role models and contributions to a particular field of study and to Christian doctrine, but the African American experience was neither expressly incorporated in the overall educational process nor in the presentation of the biblical story.

Cain Hope Felder, a contemporary African American biblical scholar, provides insight into one aspect of this failure. Highlighting the influence of European cultures on biblical interpretation, he asserts that "throughout Western history the authority of the Bible has been predicated upon the tacit assumption of the preeminence of

Teaching the Triple-Heritage through the Spirituals

European cultures."[3] Felder maintains that African American, Afro-Asiatic, Asian, and Hispanic people have typically been viewed as "secondary to the ancient biblical narratives" and that, historically, the standard by which we read and interpret the Bible has been shaped by the dominant culture.[4]

Although clear evidence exists for the presence and participation of black people in the Bible itself, many Eurocentric church leaders, administrators, and religious scholars still ignore African contributions. Consequently, these contributions have been distorted, reinterpreted, and reimaged to communicate Eurocentric characters, standards, and values.[5] Unfortunately, many African Americans have embraced and incorporated these distortions in their Bible study, worship, and religious practices. Some African American churches still display pictures that portray Jesus with long blond hair and blue eyes, and members of these congregations often become offended when asked to remove these pictures or to replace them with a black image of Jesus. They have accepted an image of Jesus that was created by the dominant culture and resist other images that may be more representative of their own experience and culture or even more accurate to a Jew from Nazareth.

Felder's insightful discussion also emphasizes the broader impact of Western cultures on African people. He clearly illustrates how African Americans have virtually been stripped of their heritage, indoctrinated with a Eurocentric worldview, and led to believe that anything Eurocentric is better than anything African. Thus, the very presence and contributions of African people, not only in the Bible, but also throughout social history, have been devalued, dehumanized, and denied. This reality has perpetuated self-hatred, lack of respect for one another, black-on-black violence, and a systematic denial of African American personhood.

Amos Wilson further illuminates Felder's argument regarding the impact of Western cultures on African people. In *Black-on-Black Violence,* Wilson presents a horrifying portrait of the social and cultural dynamics that are responsible for perpetuating black-on-black violence in America. Wilson's main focus is on the psychodynamics of white supremacy and how it has become the root cause of black-on-black violence.[6] Wilson maintains that "in the dominant White

11

American consciousness the African male is existentially guilty," which implies that he is guilty by simply "being alive."[7] In a sense, this inherent expectation creates a "self-fulfilling prophecy" that is played out in the African American male psyche and eventually in his actions.

Most striking about Wilson's discussion is his portrayal of the devastating reality of the system of black self-annihilation and the deep sense of hopelessness African Americans experience. Although Wilson offers some helpful recommendations for the preservation and empowerment of the African American community,[8] the question remains whether there is any hope. The answer can be a resounding yes if the church offers hope of communal, cultural, and moral formation for African Americans who have been cast adrift in a violent and seemingly hopeless society.

Despite the negative impact of Western culture, Christian education that is grounded in the African American triple-heritage can serve as an important corrective. Such education encourages African Americans to unashamedly embrace their triple-heritage as Africans, African Americans, and Christians and thus reflect on the reality of God throughout their unique history. As it relates to the Bible, the triple-heritage also challenges African Americans to reimage, reinterpret, and re-present the biblical story so that they may begin to see *themselves* not only as a strong and viable presence in the Bible, but also in the broader society.

If African American churches are to teach the triple-heritage effectively, they must have a viable process for experiencing, expressing, and teaching this heritage. Thus, this chapter introduces the triple-heritage model by exploring its basic components and illustrating how the spirituals can be used to explore each of them.

Defining a Triple-Heritage Model of Christian Education

The three basic components of a triple-heritage model of Christian education parallel the three aspects of the African American historical experience: African, African American, and Christian. Each component works cooperatively to present a balanced or holistic view of the triple-heritage. These components are intimately intertwined with distinctive characteristics and traditions. Consequently, as the three elements are drawn together engaging various aspects of the other components, they deepen and inform one another. In a similar fashion, the triple-heritage model of Christian education must be seen as a whole unit, with interrelated components, rather than as three separate and completely distinct elements. Diagram 1 illustrates the three major components of the model.

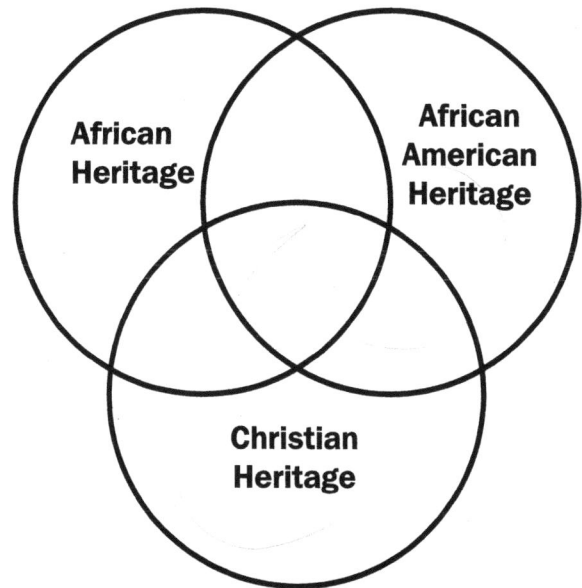

Diagram 1. Triple-Heritage Model of Christian Education—Major Components

The central point of intersection is where the spirituals draw the three components together and where the reflection upon the educational process begins. Diagram 2 on the next page illustrates how the three components of the model come together in the spirituals. The broken lines reflect the dynamic relationship among the components.

The collaborative nature of this model of Christian education can be observed through three perspectives. First, there is a collaborative relationship among the three components: African, African

Diagram 2. Triple-Heritage Model: The Spirituals at the Central Point of Intersection

American, and Christian. Second, the three components are in a collaborative relationship with the spirituals. While the spirituals are informed by the triple-heritage, they also shape the heritage. Third, educators and learners are in a collaborative relationship with the educational model. As the model influences educators and learners, those who participate in the educational process also influence and shape the model. This dynamic interchange echoes Maria Harris's notion of fashioning. In her book *Fashion Me a People*, Harris maintains that as curriculum fashions or shapes people, people in turn fashion curriculum.[9]

Purpose

The purpose of a triple-heritage model of Christian education is threefold: to allow African Americans to preserve and celebrate their full heritage as Africans, African Americans, and Christians; to explore alternative approaches to Christian education that draw upon the resources that naturally emerge from African American Christian heritage; and to present the triple-heritage in a balanced fashion throughout the curriculum so that each component is fully represented.

Curriculum Design

A triple-heritage model incorporates three essential elements of curriculum design. First, it embodies what Mary Elizabeth Moore refers to as a "planned course," or a "pathway (course) over which persons travel on a journey" of faith.[10] In the Christian context, the triple-heritage curriculum forms such a faith journey. Although Moore emphasizes the map as a metaphor for describing this planned course, she expands the metaphor to include the travelers, the guidebook, the travel plans, and the guide. She also notes that because people, places, and life circumstances are always changing, the map must be continually revised. Thus, the primary purpose of curriculum, according to Moore, is to give guidance throughout the journey of faith.[11] In a triple-heritage model, a planned course gives guidance for African Americans seeking to know more about their cultural heritage in light of their Christian faith.

Second, a triple-heritage model embraces a comprehensive view of curriculum, which includes the "entire course of the church's life."[12] Maria Harris has broadened the traditional understanding of curriculum by suggesting that curriculum includes not only formal instruction and printed materials, but also various forms of church life such as worship, fellowship, preaching, prayer, and service. She goes on to suggest that this comprehensive curriculum is intergenerational and creative, embracing multiple forms of education.[13] In a triple-heritage model, all aspects of church life are embraced as curriculum, particularly since participation in the various facets of church life has been a common mode of education in the African American church. For example, persons have typically learned to pray by participating in prayer services. Likewise, individuals have learned the spirituals and the stories of African ancestors by participating in worship. A comprehensive view of curriculum allows the church to draw upon educational opportunities that emerge whenever the church gathers in community for fellowship and nurture, as well as when the church scatters throughout the broader community in outreach and service.

Third, a triple-heritage model draws upon the oral tradition of storytelling, proverbs, folktales, music, dance, poetry, ritual, metaphor, and drumming as viable sources of curriculum. Although many African American churches have abandoned the oral tradition in favor of formal education and printed resources, Ella Mitchell argues that the oral tradition "is a legitimate system of teaching and learning" and that the African American church should not forget this valuable mode of education.[14] This system of learning, grounded in African tradition, was not only creative and fun, but it allowed African slaves to transmit important information. In a triple-heritage model, the oral tradition allows the church to draw upon resources that naturally emerge from African American tradition as viable modes of education. Furthermore, the oral tradition inspires African Americans to reclaim indigenous cultural expression throughout the educational process.

Criterion

The major criterion for a triple-heritage model of Christian education is that each aspect of the triple-heritage must be present throughout the entire educational process. Although at times one aspect may be more dominant than others, each component must be present and explored simultaneously throughout the process.

The starting point for a triple-heritage model is at the point of intersection where the three components meet through the African American spirituals. We cannot start with the notion that one aspect of the heritage is more important than the others. To do so would mean breaking up the heritage, which results in a sense of disconnectedness. Therefore, the triple-heritage must be viewed as a whole unit that cannot be separated. The spirituals help to facilitate this process by drawing the three components together at the center of the model. In the spirituals we begin to reflect on the triple-heritage as a whole unit with three interrelated parts that function cooperatively through a dynamic and integrative relationship. Although the spirituals are discussed in detail later, I offer a brief sketch of them now to illustrate how they are integrated into a triple-heritage model.

Characteristics

At least four characteristics describe a triple-heritage educational model informed by the spirituals. The model is communal, creative, critical, and cooperative.

Communal

Since the spirituals were created and sung in community, they inspire a sense of community within the educational process. This sense of community draws students and teachers together in a mutual dialogue or call-and-response. The call-and-response, commonly seen in the spirituals and grounded in African music, usually begins with a chant (that often includes a lead phrase or question), sung by a leader or member of the gathered community. The group or congregation enters the dialogue by responding to the lead phrases with statements that echo a part of the lead phrase, answer a question raised in the lead phrase, or expand the original thought. This rhythmic exchange reveals the communal nature of the spirituals. Further, it promotes a communal dialogue that encourages students and teachers both to participate fully in the educational process.

A triple-heritage model encourages dialogue not only between students and teachers, but also among religious educators, theologians, curriculum designers, and curriculum users. This model challenges them to engage in a collaborative effort to explore and integrate subject matter, curriculum themes, and educational methodology. Throughout this process, curriculum users are an integral part of the collaboration, sharing their experiences, concerns, and vision for effective curriculum design. In a triple-heritage model, educators seek to overcome the sense of disconnectedness that often characterizes educational curricula. Because each person involved in the educational process brings something valuable to the dialogue, anyone may begin the call-and-response at any time, engaging the entire community in a dynamic exchange of ideas and experiences. Consequently, everyone involved in each aspect of the educational process can help to shape the overall process, making it both assessable and more immediately relevant.

Creative

Zora Neale Hurston noted that the spirituals are always in the process of creation.[15] A common characteristic of the spirituals is improvisation, so they can be shaped and reshaped to accommodate a particular situation or event. For example, the words in the spiritual "Don' Let Nobody Turn You Aroun' " were adapted to "Don' let segregation turn you aroun' " and used during the civil rights movement in the 1960s. Freedom fighters such as Fannie Lou Hamer and Bernice Johnson Reagon were intimately involved in transforming these songs into freedom songs that ultimately undergirded the movement. These women embodied the spirit of the movement through their commitment to the survival and liberation of their people. They expressed their commitment not only through music, but also through their creative participation in the marches, rallies, and sit-ins. In a similar fashion, a triple-heritage model of Christian education is always in the process of creation. The content, practice, and participants are shaped and reshaped throughout the educational process. Drawing upon resources that naturally emerge from the African, African American, and Christian traditions, this model seeks to incorporate creative ideas, creative methodology, and creative programming.

Critical

Some spirituals possess a dual or hidden meaning that allowed the enslaved community to communicate secret messages with one another without being detected by their masters. This feature, grounded in African tradition, allowed the slave community to relate words of insult, history, wisdom, humor, and critique. For instance, the words "ev'rybody talkin' 'bout heav'n ain't goin' there" were often used to mock slaveholders and to critique their religious hypocrisy. Just as the enslaved community critiqued their world through the spirituals, a triple-heritage model seeks to engage students in a serious critique of the barriers, obstacles, systems, and structures that lead to oppression. In addition, this model seeks to empower African Americans to bring about liberation and social change by involving them in a liberative praxis that stimulates critical reflection and action within the community.

Moreover, given that many approaches to critical engagement are destructive and divisive, a triple-heritage model challenges African Americans to seek creative alternatives that unify and empower individuals within the community to struggle towards social change. These approaches may include music, dance, poetry, and other artistic expressions. Engaging these forms of artistic expression is significant because they often create a sense of community as they are expressed in community. Because the spirituals in particular are improvisational and can be adapted for various circumstances, they can be used to empower the community to speak to the immediate situation at hand. For example, when the freedom songs were sung during the civil rights movement, the community immediately came together to challenge racism, discrimination, and oppressive social systems and structures. These songs served not only as social critique, but also as a source of inspiration and motivation in the struggle towards liberation. Thus, a triple-heritage model can offer both critical and creative approaches for social analysis, reflection, and critique.

Cooperative

The desire for freedom — "O freedom! O freedom! O freedom over me!" — motivated many who were enslaved to resist the bonds of slavery. Consequently, the slave community joined together in a cooperative effort to assist in the escape of hundreds of slaves. As creations of the slave community, the spirituals became vital tools in the quest for freedom. As such, they were often used to aid in many escapes by announcing secret meetings, identifying gathering places, signaling imminent escapes, and motivating the community for action. As indicated earlier, one of the most successful efforts was the Underground Railroad led by Harriet Tubman, who also used the spirituals to facilitate numerous escapes. Thus, through cooperative action, the community creatively employed the spirituals as they united in the struggle for freedom and social change.

In a similar fashion, a triple-heritage model, grounded in the spirituals, seeks to engage African Americans in creative cooperative action to bring about transformation in their communities. The spirituals can facilitate this effort because they are inherently corporate and they have the ability to promote community. As they are sung in community, the spirituals often transcend differences of specific beliefs and backgrounds and invite greater participation from diverse populations. The spirituals thus motivate and inspire persons towards action, allowing for unity in diversity and strength in numbers. By fostering cooperative action, the spirituals, through song, challenge the church to move beyond dialogue, often confined to the church building or classrooms, to active involvement in both local and global communities, and ain't dat good news?

Notes

1. Quoted from the school's information handout.
2. Paul Hill Jr., *Coming of Age: African American Male Rites of Passage* (Chicago: African American Images, 1992), 66.
3. Cain Hope Felder, "Cultural Ideology, Afrocentrism and Biblical Interpretation," in *Black Theology: A Documentary History,* vol. 2: *1980–1992,* ed. James H. Cone and Gayraud S. Wilmore, 2nd ed. (Maryknoll, N.Y.: Orbis Books, 1993), 184.
4. Felder, "Cultural Ideology," 184–85.
5. Felder, "Cultural Ideology," 188–91.
6. Amos N. Wilson, *Black-on-Black Violence: The Psychodynamics of Black Self-Annihilation in Service of White Domination* (New York: Afrikan World Infosystems, 1990), xii–xiii, 4–10.
7. Wilson, 9.
8. Wilson, 201–5.
9. Maria Harris, *Fashion Me a People: Curriculum in the Church* (Louisville, Ky.: Westminster/John Knox Press, 1989), 17.
10. Mary Elizabeth Moore, "Rhythmic Curriculum: Guiding an Educative Journey," paper presented in the symposium Les Rythmes Educatifs dans la Philosophie de Whitehead, Université Catholique de Lille, Lille, France, April 25–27, 1994, 11.
11. Moore, 11.
12. Maria Harris, *Fashion Me a People,* 17.
13. Maria Harris, *Fashion Me a People,* 17–18.
14. Ella Mitchell, 98, 111–12.
15. Zora Neale Hurston, "Spirituals and Neo-Spirituals," in *The Negro in Music and Art,* ed. Lindsay Patterson, International Library of Negro Life and History (1933; reprint, New York: Publishers Company, 1967), 15.

Two

Deep River

Exploring the Triple-Heritage

To teach the triple-heritage effectively, African Americans must have a clear understanding of its individual components as well as their synthesis into an interrelated whole. Thus, the purpose of this chapter is to define the triple-heritage in more detail, beginning with a brief discussion of its holistic nature and then proceeding with an analysis of each element.

A Holistic View

I first encountered the term "triple-heritage"[1] at the First Institutional Baptist Church of Phoenix, Arizona, under the leadership of Warren H. Stewart Sr. It had emerged as a part of the vision for the African American Christian Training School (AACTS), a biweekly Saturday school designed to teach black children and youth about their heritage as Africans, Americans, and Christians. The purpose of AACTS is to "transform and produce generations of children and youth through a Triple-Heritage Model: thusly, [sic] producing adults that are proud of their African, American and Christian heritages...."[2]

The triple-heritage, as envisioned through the AACTS ministry, refers to the African, American, and Christian heritage. According to the Reverend Jackie L. Green, the former director of AACTS, youth must know who they are as Africans to appreciate the contributions that African people have made to society; youth must know who they are as Americans to claim ownership of this country, especially since this country was built upon the backs of African foreparents; and youth must know who they are as Christians to affirm their uniqueness as children of God and to live their lives fully and completely for Christ.[3]

I would like to broaden the AACTS definition of the African component of the triple-heritage by assuming a wider global (Pan-African) perspective that includes all persons of African descent, whether on the continent of Africa or in other parts of the world. I also make a distinction between American heritage and African American heritage.[4] Although the African American experience is a part of the American heritage, I believe there is a danger of losing the distinctiveness of the African American experience when this aspect of the triple-heritage is identified only as American. Furthermore, the AACTS understanding of the Christian component of the triple-heritage is expanded by reflecting specifically on the Christian experience of African Americans, lifting up the uniqueness of African American Christianity.

Components of the Triple-Heritage

Because the triple-heritage must be viewed as a whole, a clear understanding of each aspect of the triple-heritage is vital to this holistic concept of the African American Christian heritage.

African Heritage

African heritage refers to the history, culture, and geography of Africa and African peoples in the Diaspora. Embracing African heritage enables African Americans to value who they are as African people and compels them to stand in solidarity with all of their sisters and brothers of African descent in the struggle for liberation. Part of the problem, however, is that not only are African Americans uninformed about Africa, but they often reject it as the "source of their ancestral heritage"[5] and deny the value of anything African.

The rejection of Africanness has been perpetuated historically through the false notion that African beliefs, values, and practices are "pagan," "uncivilized," and thus "undesirable." Henry Mitchell sheds light on how these images of Africanness have affected African Americans through the years. He notes: "In time what our ancestors knew to be African and 'proper' was viewed as African and 'pagan' or 'ignorant.' After that it was seen as just 'Black' and 'undesirable' with consequent psychological damages to Black self-esteem."[6] The church's task, then, is not only to inform about Africa, but also to help redefine what is meant by African heritage.

The assault on African American self-esteem and self-acceptance has been waged on many fronts. I'd like to explore four particularly powerful assaults and suggest ways the church can respond to them.

The first assault is that African traditional practices and beliefs have been devalued. Although the first Africans arrived in this country with a rich heritage that included a dynamic worldview, diverse cultural practices, and a vibrant religious tradition, the white slave owners, missionaries, and other supporters of slavery failed to recognize the value of their African background. Negative connotations and characteristics were assigned to African practices and beliefs, thus demeaning all aspects of African life. For instance, during the time of slavery, white American society refused to acknowledge the existence of an indigenous African culture and civilization, perpetuating the myth that Africans were ignorant, uncivilized heathens who needed to be bound, broken, and tamed, thereby justifying the enslavement and continued exploitation of African people.

Traditional African religious beliefs and practices were considered pagan and superstitious. For example, since Africans have a great respect for all of nature, including the sun, moon, stars, wind, rivers, trees, and animals, they were accused of "animism" and "nature worship," practices viewed by the missionaries as idolatrous. Accompanying this was the widespread notion that Africans have no concept of a Supreme Being. This belief has led to a disrespect of the African understanding of God and has perpetuated the notion that Africans worship the devil and fetishes.[8] But such accusations are clearly wrong. The African understanding of God betrays both subtlety and complexity, a fact that, ironically, was overlooked perhaps because of the missionaries' own prejudice and lack of sophistication.

The African understanding of community has also been rejected in favor of an individualistic society that stresses the protection of private property and individual rights as the basis for social and political organization. Traditionally, the African community has been characterized by extended families that provide social, economic, and spiritual support. Africans have typically relied upon this communal support system for assistance with children and family concerns, emotional strength and encouragement, spiritual guidance and direction, consultation for legal and economic matters, fraternal affiliations, and communal and tribal identity.[9] A strong emphasis on individualism in the United States has led to the breakdown of the African American family, the social crisis within the African American community, and the lack of positive transmission of familial, cultural, and Christian values.[10] Consequently, many African American youth are turning to street values for guidance, support, and direction.

Nigerian educator A. Okechukwu Ogbonnaya suggests that balance between the individual and the community is central to an African concept of community. He maintains that "the individual is primarily connected to others psychically, spiritually, and physically, and second, a "for-her/himself" individual. Even in one's individuality one is never truly separated from his or her fundamental communal connection."[11] This view of community suggests a mutual relationship that allows persons to be concerned about the well-being of others in relation to self as each person strives to maintain harmony within the community. This fundamental understanding of community has virtually disappeared in American society.

Perhaps the ultimate devaluation of African culture is that African practices have been replaced by European American norms and conventions. This was particularly evident during the time of slavery when Africans were prohibited from using their native language and forced to adopt English. Africans were also stripped of their African names and given new names by their slave masters. Furthermore, they were forced to learn new work skills that would aid them in the daily rigors of planting and harvesting cotton, sugar cane, and other staple crops.[12] Although a new way of life, a new view of the world, and new modes of communication surrounded African slaves, Gayraud Wilmore argues that Africans "defied total assimilation" and fought to maintain some level of their African identity.[13] Nevertheless, the practice of replacing African modes of life with European American norms and conventions, initially employed to "season" or break Africans into the harsh realities of plantation life,[14] served to perpetuate the myth that Africanness is less than desirable.

The second assault on African American self-esteem and self-acceptance emerges from the understanding of "black" as evil, bad, and dirty, and "white" as good, pure, and clean. Over the years, negative images of blackness have been perpetuated in everyday experiences and promoted through music, art, literature, media, education, science, history, and religious teachings. In the article published by the Kelly Miller Smith Institute entitled "What Does It Mean to Be Black and Christian?" we find a striking illustration of how these images have been understood by society. In this discussion, the terms "black" and "white" are presented as they have been defined in Webster's Third New International Dictionary.[15] Some of the definitions given under each word are presented below.

> *white* — free from blemish, moral stain or impurity; outstandingly righteous; innocent; not marked by malignant influence; notably pleasing as auspicious; fortunate; notably ardent; decent; in a fair and uprightly manner; a sterling man.
>
> *black* — outrageously wicked, a villain; dishonorable; expressing or indicating disgrace, discredit or guilt; connected with the devil; expressing menace; sullen; hostile; unqualified; committing a violation of public regulation; illicit, illegal; affected by some undesirable condition.[16]

In her analysis of the differences between "blackness" and "whiteness," Delores Williams notes that disparaging images of the color black have been perpetuated through scientific, religious, and political arenas. This negative understanding of blackness has contributed to the assault on African American personhood and the continued oppression of African American people.[17]

The rejection of African standards of beauty and the imposition of negative myths and stereotypes upon African American people constitute the third assault on African American self-esteem and self-acceptance. Because black is viewed as inherently bad, African features and characteristics have also been considered less than desirable. Just as black personhood has been considered inferior, so have African standards of beauty. A childhood chant illustrates the subtle message of black inferiority.

> If you're white you're all right,
> if you're yellow you're mellow,
> if you're brown stick around,
> if you're black you better get back.[18]

Like many African Americans, I heard this chant recited by both black and white children. The message of white superiority and black inferiority has been ingrained in American consciousness, resulting in negative myths, stereotypes, and beliefs about African American humanity, ethnicity, and sexuality.

The fourth assault on African American self-esteem and self-acceptance is that African history has been portrayed negatively or ignored altogether in American history. Throughout American history, Africans have typically been presented as ignorant savages who had no cultural background and who were virtually uncivilized until they came into contact with European people; enslaved Africans were considered the lower class, uneducated outcasts of society. Leonard Barrett maintains along with Melville Herskovits that it was precisely this view of Africans as inferior that formed the premise for the "moral code" that governed European interaction with the slaves. Racism and discrimination are the result of this myth that continues to some extent even today.[19]

Confronted with widespread attacks on Africanness, many African Americans have become uninterested in Africa and prefer not to embrace their African heritage. The church must become involved in correcting negative influences and assisting African Americans in seeing their African heritage in a positive light. Although the assault on African American self-esteem and self-acceptance has been great, significant work is currently being done to encourage African Americans to reclaim their African heritage and to appreciate the uniqueness of who they are as African people. Two important attempts to help people embrace their African heritage are Pan-Africanism and Afrocentrism.

Pan-Africanism

According to Sid Lemelle, "Pan-Africanism includes all people of African ancestry living in continental Africa and throughout the world."[20] Although Pan-Africanism has had a long and varied history, its primary focus has been to encourage African people to reclaim their African identity, to celebrate African culture and traditions, and to unite in the struggle for freedom and equality. Pan-Africanism embraced both a cultural and a political emphasis that eventually motivated black people to strive for political empowerment, economic freedom, and human rights. Lemelle calls attention to these cultural and political dimensions of the struggle:

> The initial thrust of the movement was to restore Black people's cultural identity by glorifying the African past: the history of great kingdoms, wise rulers and untold wealth. Pan-Africanist [sic] praised the kingdoms of Western Sudan: Ghana, Mali and Songhai, wise rulers like Mansa Musa (1312–1337), Sonni Ali (1464–1492) and Askia Mohammad (1493–1529), and the wealth of Ancient Egypt and Mwana Matapa. Throughout the history of slavery in the Americas, Africans fought to maintain their identity and dignity. Pan-Africanism is rooted in that struggle.[21]

Although there are various perspectives of Pan-Africanism, Lemelle lists several common themes that are typically emphasized through Pan-Africanism in an effort to reclaim African heritage:

- Africans and persons of African origin recognize Africa as their homeland.
- Solidarity among men and women of African descent
- Belief in a distinct "African personality"
- Restoration of Africa's history
- Pride in African cultural heritage
- Africa for Africans in church and state
- The hope for a glorious and united future Africa.[22]

Teaching the triple-heritage must involve a conscious effort to embrace and appreciate a rich African heritage and sensitivity to the struggle for liberation for all persons of African descent. Pan-Africanism can assist the African American church in this endeavor.

Afrocentrism

Afrocentrism is another movement aimed at assisting African Americans in embracing and appreciating their African heritage. Afrocentrism means to move Africa and African ideals to the central point of reflection, analysis, and critique of African American life. It is the lens through which African Americans view their history, culture, and contributions.[23]

Pan-Africanism and Afrocentrism have similar qualities in that they both acknowledge the centrality of Africa, they value African culture, they celebrate the contributions of African people, and they emphasize liberation for all persons of African descent. On the other hand, they are two distinct historical movements. Pan-Africanism has a much longer history, dating back to 1441, when Antam Goncalvez, the Portuguese explorer, enslaved twelve Africans. Although Pan-Africanism was not formally organized at that time, the struggle for liberation and the impetus to maintain African identity and heritage had begun.[24] Pan-Africanism emphasized and continues to promote a strong global focus, political orientation, and active participation in the liberation of all African people.

Afrocentrism, in contrast, is a recent movement that has emerged during the late twentieth century. Although Afrocentrism also incorporates a global, political, and liberative orientation, it tends to place a greater emphasis on cultural and historical concerns.

Molefi Kete Asante, of Temple University, coined the term "Afrocentricity" in 1980[25] in an effort to combat negative images of Africa and the denial of African contributions to society. According to Asante, Afrocentricity is a particular orientation to data that centers on the beauty of Africa and acknowledges Africans as "subjects of historical and social experiences rather than objects in the margins of European experiences."[26] Consequently, Afrocentricity esteems African heritage, inspiring a sense of appreciation and pride. Asante's work is significant in that he removes Europe as the central focus, placing Africa at the heart of African American consciousness.

Although Afrocentrism supports global solidarity (though not as strongly as Pan-Africanism) in the effort to liberate all persons of African descent from economic, political, and racial oppression, it is particularly valuable for African Americans because it encourages them to reclaim a sense of pride in their African heritage and in the contributions that their African ancestors have made. Afrocentrism is a powerful reminder to African Americans that they are significant and that they are capable of advancing the well-being of this society. Thus, Afrocentrism's assertion that African people have participated in the world community throughout history, as fully engaged subjects rather than quiescent objects, is a source of motivation and inspiration for many African Americans.

Afrocentrism allows African Americans to embrace their triple-heritage by providing what Asante refers to as a metatheoretical framework that moves them through three basic stages: dislocation — having no sense of historical awareness or consciousness, resulting in a devaluing of the African heritage; location — identifying their orientation with regard to Afrocentricity and Eurocentricity; and relocation — recovering, reclaiming, and revaluing their African heritage.[27]

Pan-Africanism and Afrocentrism can both assist the church in focusing on African heritage by affirming, celebrating, and embracing Africa as the ancestral heritage of African Americans.

African American Heritage

African American heritage refers to the experience, culture, and significant contributions of African Americans in the United States. The African American component of the triple-heritage encourages African Americans to affirm their personhood, to celebrate their historical contributions, and to value all aspects of their rich heritage as African Americans. This holistic understanding of African American heritage is significant because African Americans are not just African and they are not just American, but they are both African and American, and they have a developed tradition as African Americans. When African Americans embrace their full heritage, they can appreciate the uniqueness of who they really are. With this in mind, the aim of the African American component is threefold: to teach African Americans about their heritage, to create an appreciation for this heritage, and to encourage a sense of responsibility to the African American community.

Many African Americans today know little about their heritage. While some are familiar with a number of celebrities and sports personalities, many of them have a limited understanding of African American history and are virtually unaware of the struggles and significant contributions made by African American people. This lack of knowledge has resulted in a lack of pride in African American heritage and a lack of hope and direction for the future. Through triple-heritage curriculum, African-focused celebrations, and attention to distinctly African American worship space and styles, the church can assist African Americans in reclaiming a sense of pride in their African American heritage.

I'd like to explore the African American component of the triple-heritage from two major perspectives: the African American legacy of survival and liberation in the United States and the celebration of African American heroes and heroines. Although it is widely acknowledged that African American experience is diverse and multidimensional, it is important to note that African Americans in the United States share a common experience that has included a history of slavery, racism, and oppression on the one hand, and a heritage of creative expression and acts of bravery and self-sacrifice on the other.

African American Legacy of Survival and Liberation

Although the African American experience in the United States has been one of racism and oppression, the church has been, and can be, instrumental in moving African Americans towards a positive view of African American heritage. What is important to the future is not only scrutinizing the harsh realities of slavery, Jim Crow practices, violence, racism, and denial of human/civil rights of African Americans in this country, but also examining the creative ways that African Americans have overcome gross mistreatment and injustice in light of these realities. One way of doing this is to explore the African American legacy of survival and liberation.

The survival and liberation strategies of African Americans can be observed in two types of activities that African Americans have employed: resistance and protest. Resistance was actually more prevalent than commonly realized. Unaware of this fact, many African Americans have rejected their African American heritage because they have been led to believe that their history began in slavery, and is thus important to forget, and that the Africans who were brought to this country acquiesced to a life of bondage and thus left a shameful heritage. The literature, however, abounds with evidence of the Africans' refusal to accept their status as slaves. Indeed, a spirit of resistance emerged from the beginning of the slave trade and persisted until the end of slavery.[28] The slaves were quite ingenious in devising various schemes and devices for resisting the bonds of slavery.

This resistance took place on several different levels: individual, collective, and religious. On an individual level, many slaves resisted slavery by running away, refusing to work, procrastinating on the job, performing their work poorly, complaining of mysterious illnesses, refusing medication, and starving themselves.[29] On many occasions, slaves were known to attempt suicide in a number of ways. For example, Herskovits tells of a man who attempted to cut his throat after being sold into slavery. When the ship's surgeon tried to sew him up he tore out the stitches with his fingernails. He eventually died of starvation.[30] Another trader observed that the African captives were "so wilful and loth to leave their own country, that they have often leap'd out of the canoes, boat and ship, into the sea, and kept under water till they were drowned."[31] Barrett notes that many slaves committed suicide by ingesting poisons made from various herbs or arsenic. Many also committed infanticide to spare their children a life of bondage.[32]

On a collective level, many slaves resisted slavery by aiding in the escape of hundreds of slaves. Others such as Gabriel Prosser (1800), Denmark Vesey (1822), and Nat Turner (1831) initiated slave insurrections and revolts. As a whole, the slave community created an elaborate system of survival and resistance that allowed them to maintain some level of protection and solidarity. To this end, the slave community incorporated several practices including protecting one another's confidence; incorporating secret modes of communication, "taking" and not "stealing" from their masters what they believed was rightfully theirs (e.g., food items and other basic necessities); instilling within children the determination to fight the abuses of slavery; and interacting more genuinely with one another than with their masters.[33]

Religious resistance consisted of rebellion against the hypocritical teachings of white religion regarding stealing, laziness, or disclosure of another slave's whereabouts or activities. This form of resistance required a great deal of time and energy from the white preachers who tried to no avail to convince the slaves of their misdeeds. Henry Mitchell notes, however, that the most direct form of religious resistance was exemplified in the clandestine worship services that inspired the faith community to pray persistently against a system of evil and oppression as well as the slave preachers' determination to continue preaching a message of hope and freedom, even though many were beaten, tortured, and killed.[34]

The African slaves were convinced that slavery was not ordained by God and that they were created for freedom, not bondage. This message of their God-given personhood allowed the slaves to assert their human dignity through various modes of resistance that constantly inspired them to strive for liberation from an inhumane system of oppression.

Another strategy that African Americans have employed to overcome racism and oppression is active engagement in protest for liberation. A contemporary example of African American protest in the United States is the civil rights movement of the 1950s and 1960s. This movement was a massive nonviolent effort to fight for equality, civil rights, and human dignity in America.

While not without its flaws and critics, particularly from proponents of the black power movement, which emerged as a result of its failures and limitations, the civil rights movement remains an important symbol of the African American tradition of protest and struggle.

Celebration of African American Heroes and Heroines

Traditionally, American history has primarily lifted up white heroes and heroines, such as George Washington, Abraham Lincoln, Thomas Jefferson, Franklin D. Roosevelt, Eleanor Roosevelt, and

Susan B. Anthony, while countless African American heroes and heroines have been virtually ignored. Consequently, many African Americans are generally unaware of the noteworthy contributions made by remarkable African Americans. Although scholarship in this area is increasing, numerous stories of African American role models remain, for the most part, untold. The African American component of the triple-heritage can assist African Americans in celebrating their stories.

Fictional heroes/heroines appear frequently in African American folktales and children's literature. These figures are often animal characters or tricksters who are skilled at outwitting the dominant system of authority, unusual predicaments, or other fictional characters. Arna Bontemps affirms that storytelling was an integral part of African culture transported to the New World by the slaves and that the use of animal characters was a common African practice.[35] In describing the transformation of these characters from African to African American tales, Bontemps explains:

> In the African prototypes of the American Negro tales the heroes were generally the jackal, the hare, the tortoise, and the spider. The African jackal survived as the American fox, the African hare as the American rabbit, and the African tortoise as the American dry-land turtle or terrapin. The spider came only as near as the West Indies, where it reappeared in the Anansi tales of Jamaica. As a villain the African hyena was replaced by the American wolf, but that role is sometimes assigned to the fox or the bear in the American tale. The rest of the cast of characters, the lions, leopards, tigers, and monkeys, was safely transported.[36]

One of the most popular animal heroes in African American folktales is Brer Rabbit. Although the rabbit is often perceived as a "frightened" and "helpless" animal, the slaves portrayed Brer Rabbit as a cunning character who was a "practical joker, a braggart, a wit, a glutton, a lady's man, and a trickster."[37] Lawrence Levine notes that the trickster characteristic of Brer Rabbit emerged initially during the time of slavery and continued for years, in various forms, as African Americans endured various forms of oppression and injustice.[38]

Brer Rabbit was a symbol of good transcending evil or weakness overcoming strength through creative and cunning actions. He was not only celebrated for his unusual feats, but also for the important lessons regarding survival, caution, and wise counsel that emerged from his adventures.

Another fictional hero in African American folklore is High John de Conqueror. Like many African American fictional folktale heroes, he was endowed with superhuman powers that enabled him to engage in phenomenal exploits, including being transformed into other creatures, to escape peril, often at the hands of the slave master.[39] Like Brer Rabbit, John was celebrated not only for his creativity in overcoming harrowing predicaments, but also for his ability to survive in the midst of danger. The introductory comments of one folktale featuring John illustrate a great respect for his ability to survive.

> Way back during slavery time, there was a man named John. High John the Conqueror, they called him. And he was what you call a *man*. Now some folks say he was a big man, but the way I heard it, he wasn't no bigger than average height and didn't look no different than the average man. Didn't make any difference, though. He was what you call a *be* man — be here when the hard times come, and be here when the hard times are gone. No matter how much the white folks put on him, John always survived.[40]

African American fictional heroes provided a vehicle for African Americans to confront the dominant culture. These heroes not only enabled them to express their frustrations, hostilities, and aspirations, but they also allowed them to transcend their oppressive situations.

Another type of African American hero/heroine is the slave hero. While some slave heroes were fictional, many were real people, such as Harriet Tubman, Sojourner Truth, and Frederick Douglass, who actually lived through slavery. Stories of these heroes/heroines survived for years after the emancipation. Levine notes that although the history of slavery was difficult for many African Americans to recall, these stories were shared "not with defensiveness and shame but eagerly and often with pride."[41] These stories were significant for several reasons. Besides evoking deep emotion and containing important facts about slavery, they also offered insights into a unique culture of survival and resistance, providing positive portrayals of slave heroes and their creative opposition to slavery.

The stories of slave heroes/heroines can be a source of inspiration and pride for African Americans, particularly since many of these stories present a positive and realistic view of enslaved African and African American ancestors. Although many of the slave stories portray a positive view of African American slaves, Levine notes that many stories also provide a balanced view of slave character, including images of slaves such as "the craven, the sycophants, the foolish, the ruthless who preyed upon their own group."[42] But this concern for accuracy can only serve to reinforce the exploits of the slave heroes/heroines whose inspiring stories encourage respect, dignity, sacrifice, confidence, and pride in African American heritage.

The third type of African American hero/heroine is contemporary real-life persons. This group includes African Americans who have overcome tremendous odds, fought for their rights and the rights of others, and made significant contributions to society as a whole. Joe Louis, Jesse Owens and Wilma Randolph, and Jackie Robinson are examples of African American sports heroes who overcame racial barriers and excelled in their respective sports (boxing, track and field, and baseball), despite negative myths and stereotypes about African Americans and a Jim Crow system of injustice and segregation. Ida B. Wells-Barnett, Medgar Evers, and Martin Luther King Jr. are examples of heroes/heroines who fought for the rights of African Americans as well as the rights of all who are oppressed.

Beyond sports and the civil rights movement, which tend to be areas where African American heroes/heroines are most often recognized, African Americans have also made significant contributions in a variety of arenas including education, medicine, politics, law, literature, entertainment, art, religion, and science. Some of these heroes/heroines include: Maria Stewart and W. E. B. Du Bois (education); Charles Drew (medicine); Shirley Chisholm, Barbara Jordan, and Adam Clayton Powell Sr. and Jr. (politics); Thurgood Marshall (law); Maya Angelou and Nikki Giovanni (literature); Ruby Dee and Ossie Davis (fine arts); Alvin Ailey and Pearl Primus (dance); Jarena Lee and Richard Allen (religion); and Zora Neale Hurston (anthropology). Although some of the names are well known in the African American community, many others are not. The African American component of the triple-heritage can assist African Americans in exploring the unique contributions that African Americans (in public or private life) have made throughout society.

Some efforts have been made to celebrate African American heritage through Black History Month, the Martin Luther King Jr. Holiday, and Kwanzaa. However, these events only call African Americans to reflect upon their heritage periodically throughout the year. One day, one week, or one month is not sufficient for a triple-heritage model of Christian education. The African American component of the triple-heritage can assist African Americans in building a positive sense of self-worth by reflecting upon their heritage year-round and celebrating the positive contributions of African American people.

Christian Heritage

The Christian heritage embodies the whole of Christian experience, which includes the Scriptures, the traditional hymns, the creeds of the church, the prayers of the people, the ritual practices, and all aspects of the Christian tradition. The Christian component of the triple-heritage inspires African Americans to celebrate both the fullness of their Christian faith and the distinctiveness of their African American Christian heritage. By celebrating this unique heritage, African American Christians have the freedom to embrace their Christian faith without denying their African and African American roots. Thus, the AACTS objective of the Christian component of the triple-heritage is expanded to include not only "a positive understanding of the Biblical concept of humankind as God's family,"[43] but also an acknowledgment of the particular experiences of African Americans in the United States that have shaped a distinctive African American Christianity. This distinctive African American Christian heritage, according to Dr. J. Alfred Smith, a noted scholar and gifted homiletician in the African American church, was "forged in the context of suffering and oppression."[44]

Given that the unique religious experience of African Americans is often perceived as irrelevant and insignificant, the church can be instrumental in assisting African Americans in affirming their distinctive Christian heritage as a viable and legitimate expression of their Christian faith. This affirmation can be done in at least two ways: first, by putting in a positive light various aspects of African American religious experiences that have shaped a distinctive African American Christian heritage; and second, by reclaiming Christian themes commonly emphasized in the African American church that have played a significant role in promoting the survival and well-being of African Americans and their communities.

Distinctive Elements of African American Christian Heritage

Four distinctive elements of the African American church are considered here: slave religion, theology, worship, and the role of the church. These elements are important because they embody some of the nuances of African American Christian faith, and they are still prominent in the African American church today.

Slave Religion. One of the most distinctive features of African American Christianity is the history of enslavement. While many would prefer to ignore this aspect, others contend that African American Christian heritage can only be fully understood when examined in the context of slavery. Through the experience of slavery, along with the synthesis of traditional African religions and Christianity, a distinctive Christian faith emerged among the slaves that enabled them to survive under the brutal system of chattel slavery, which denied their humanity and devalued their African heritage.[45] This faith, born out of suffering, underscored freedom, human dignity, resistance to bondage, and the ultimate justice of God. By beginning with an examination of the unique Christian faith or "slave religion" created by the slaves, African Americans can gain insight into the culture of the slaves and the creative strategies that they employed not only to survive, but also to resist their condition of bondage.

Three aspects of slave religion inform our discussion on the distinctiveness of African American Christian heritage. One aspect is that slaves valued their secret religious meetings as a place of refuge, as social gatherings, and as a means of freedom of expression. These secret meetings, commonly referred to as the "invisible institution," allowed the slaves to gather together and to worship God in their own

Deep River

way, free from the presence and dictates of the white slave owners. Although these meetings were often prohibited and could ultimately result in severe punishment or death, the slaves continued to find solace in their sacred time together.

Slaves also had a unique interpretation of God, Jesus, and human worth. Although they were in bondage, the slaves saw themselves as "children of God." Identifying closely with the children of Israel and the Exodus story, the slaves embraced a vision of God as a deliverer of the oppressed. Jesus was viewed not only as a suffering servant and friend, who understood what it meant to be oppressed, but also as a conquering king who, through the power of his resurrection, could overcome even the most oppressive structures. The slaves believed that they were valued in the eyes of God and that, one day, they too would be delivered from their bondage.[46] This self-understanding created a deepened sense of self-worth and inspired the slave community to strengthen its resolve to resist the bonds of slavery and to continue in its struggle towards liberation.

The slaves, moreover, enjoyed spontaneous, high-spirited worship services, which consisted of preaching, praying, singing, shouting, dancing, and fellowship. Although these elements of worship were common in the slave community, other traditional elements such as the call to worship and the invitation to discipleship were equally important. In addition, the slave community relied upon the oral tradition of singing to gather the worshiping community or to communicate among themselves, storytelling as a form of preaching and teaching, and proverbs as a mode of sharing their wisdom and their faith.[47]

Slave religion is a distinctive aspect of African American Christianity. Although some of the religious practices common in the invisible institution have been lost over time, many of these features are still present in African American Christianity today.

Theology. Another distinctive feature of African American Christian heritage is the African American theology of God, Jesus, humanity, and freedom. African American scholars generally agree that racism and oppression have significantly influenced African American interpretations of these elements. Although African Americans typically embrace the same traditional beliefs as white Christians,

Exploring the Triple-Heritage

their experience of racism and oppression uniquely shapes the particular focus and emphasis placed upon these theological themes. For instance, as C. Eric Lincoln and Lawrence M. Mamiya correctly observe, a common view of God in the African American church is that of an avenger, conqueror, and deliverer, working on behalf of those who are oppressed and downtrodden. This dynamic conception of God is vividly portrayed in the Old Testament. African Americans also embrace a concrete rather than an abstract notion of Jesus, stressing his humanity along with his divinity and personal concern for their well-being. In this context, the suffering, death, and resurrection of Jesus are commonly emphasized in light of the African American experience of racism and oppression. Thus, African Americans identify with Jesus through his human experience of suffering and find hope of liberation through his victorious resurrection.[48]

Racism and oppression have also affected African American interpretations of humanity and freedom. Since the first African slaves arrived in the New World, African Americans have struggled to affirm their self-worth and humanity. Although the systems of slavery, racism, and oppression have refused to affirm them as fully human, African Americans have embraced a vision of their human acceptance and value in the eyes of God. Grounded in their unique theological interpretations, African Americans have historically emphasized this vision of humanity and persisted in their belief that they are indeed children of God, created in freedom, and a valued part of the human family.[49]

Over the years, the African American church has affirmed the biblical understanding of human freedom and has inspired African Americans to strive for freedom in every aspect of their lives. As the plight of African Americans has changed over time, however, the emphasis and subsequent meaning of freedom has also shifted accordingly. In their insightful study of the African American church, Lincoln and Mamiya shed light on this progression. For example, slavery brought about an emphasis on freedom from bondage. After the emancipation, the emphasis shifted to freedom of education, employment, and full participation in society. Most recently, during the twentieth and twenty-first centuries, the emphasis on freedom has included the struggle for justice in social, political, and economic arenas.[50]

Worship. Worship is the third distinctive feature of African American Christian heritage. African American worship is a celebration of God's active involvement through the incarnate Christ among the people of God in their struggle for justice and liberation. Although worship (corporate and personal) is an important part of all Christian congregations, African American churches embody a distinctive quality and character, which emerge out of the historical context and particular experience of African Americans.[51]

Worship in the African American experience has long been concerned with the holistic needs of the congregation and wider community. While emphasizing the spiritual nurture and development of its members, worship in many African American churches has also included attention to various cultural concerns such as social analysis and critique, affirmation of African American heritage, and inspiration for active involvement in the struggle towards liberation and social change. In addition to the cultural concerns of African American worship, three other elements, as creatively expressed in the African American experience, have often been recognized as "uniquely African American."[52] These elements include music, preaching, and prayer. For example, music in the African American church is central to the spiritual expression of African Americans, allowing them to share their deepest cares and concerns, born out of their particular experience of oppression. Encompassing many forms, including African American spirituals, gospel music, and meter hymns, music in the African American church is often emotional, spontaneous, celebrative, and expressive.[53]

Preaching in African American worship is often characterized as dialogical, whereby the preacher and congregation engage in a verbal interchange or "call-and-response." Other common characteristics of African American preaching are teaching and storytelling. The primary aim of the preaching moment, however, is to inspire a deeper faith and sense of spirituality among the worshiping community.[54]

Prayer in African American worship is significant in that it allows African Americans to express their faith in God, affirm their personhood as children of God, and embrace a sense of hope and healing in the midst of oppression. In this context, prayer embodies several unique qualities that have been shaped by the particular experience

Exploring the Triple-Heritage

of African Americans. First, it incorporates metaphoric prayer language, which often expresses the African American experience of suffering and oppression. Second, it is spontaneous and free flowing, indicating, for many African Americans, a sense of spirituality and empowerment by the Holy Spirit. Third, prayer is often expressed melodically or rhythmically. This form of praying (and sometimes preaching) is often referred to as "tuning." Fourth, prayer is communal, lifting up the cares and concerns of the worshiping community. Fifth, prayer is often accompanied by praise, which helps to prepare the congregation for worship and ushers in the presence of the Holy Spirit. Finally, prayer in the African American church embodies an element of "holy boldness" (approaching God confidently), which reflects the steadfast faith of the worshiping community.[55]

The presence of the Holy Spirit is another significant aspect of worship in the African American church. Indeed, the Holy Spirit inspires the worship celebration while providing wisdom and comfort for the worshiping community. The Spirit also empowers the congregation as well as individual worshipers as they move towards personal and communal transformation. As the community engages in worship, the movement of the Holy Spirit can be a dynamic experience for individuals and may evoke a wide range of responses from "the silent rapt countenance or the low murmur and moan to the mad abandon of physical fervor, — the stamping, shrieking, and shouting, the rushing to and fro and wild waving of arms, the weeping and laughing, the vision and the trance."[56]

The most dramatic of these responses, still common in many African American churches, is known as the "frenzy." The frenzy, according to W. E. B. Du Bois, was the high-spirited response or "shouting" of some worshipers when they "got the Spirit" and were filled with an overwhelming joy.[57] For many worshipers, the frenzy was concrete evidence of the presence of God among them. Although shouting is not characteristic of all African American churches, the movement of the Holy Spirit is a vital part of the African American worship experience. The distinctive elements of worship in the African American church continue to affirm for many African Americans that worship in the African American experience is deeply rooted in African heritage and shaped by the religious experience of the slave community.

41

Role of the Church. The last distinctive feature of African American Christian heritage is the central role of the church. From its inception, the African American church has played a vital role in empowering African American people. Since African Americans have been denied full participation in the broader society, the church has become the center of the African American community, giving rise to numerous businesses, organizations, and institutions. The African American church has also been the focal point of political, social, and cultural activity promoting a sense of hope and inspiration, which has challenged African Americans to continue in their struggle for justice and liberation. Reflecting upon the legacy of the African American church, Olivia Pearl Stokes captures the essence of the church's impact on the African American community. She maintains that the African American church has been "the communities' protest center, the spiritual powerhouse, and the fellowship community center for radical unity, talent launching, and fund raising for survival causes."[58] Through the church, which has served both a spiritual and social role, African Americans have been able to participate fully in the African American community.

The African American church has also been a sanctuary for healing and wholeness. African Americans have long believed that the high-spirited nature of some African American worship services provides a safe place for African Americans to express their deepest cares and concerns. Many in the black community embrace this freedom of expression as a source of emotional and psychological healing for those confronted not only by the daily challenges of life, but also by the burdens of racism, oppression, disenfranchisement, and various forms of discrimination and injustice. The church also challenges African Americans to take an active role in transforming their personal and communal lives through self-care, community involvement, and social action. Thus, in the ongoing struggle for justice and liberation, the church enables African Americans to function in a hostile world. To this end, the African American church emphasizes both faith and action while ministering to the individual and communal needs of the entire congregation.[59]

The African American church has been, and still is, the place where suffering people come to release their emotions and renew their "hopes, faith, and courage."[60] This unique experience has inspired African Americans to continue in the struggle for liberation.

Finally, the African American church has played a vital role in the education of African Americans. Prior to the emancipation, scores of African Americans were systematically denied their right to freedom and education. Consequently, the church became the focal point of education and leadership development in the black community. Because formal educational resources were not readily available to African Americans, they relied primarily upon the Bible and whatever resources they could obtain to educate themselves.[61] Although the focus of education in contemporary African American churches has shifted more towards spiritual formation, education continues to be an important emphasis in the African American community.

African Americans' experience of Christianity is distinctive in that various aspects of slave religion, African American theological interpretations, indigenous worship styles, and the unique role of the African American church have shaped it.

Reclaiming Christian Themes in the African American Church

In addition to these distinctive religious experiences, African American Christianity may also be understood in terms of the themes commonly advanced in the African American church. Three in particular, faith, love, and service, are examined here. These themes appear throughout the life of the African American church in the preached Word, the teaching of the biblical text, the congregational and choral singing, and the prayers of the people.[62] Furthermore, these themes have played a significant role in the psychological, social, and spiritual survival of African American people. Over the years, a strong faith in God, love for self and others, pride in the African American heritage, and a sense of responsibility to the community have allowed some African Americans to overcome the effects of racism and oppression and to transform their communities.

Historically, the African American church has played a significant role in *shaping the faith of African American people*. In recent years, however, the church's influence on contemporary African Americans has sharply declined. In light of this alarming trend, the task of the African American church is to inspire a renewed sense of faith in God among African Americans that is relevant, liberative, and transformative.

A renewed sense of faith in God is vital to the African American church because God is still embraced in this community as a God of love, justice, survival, and liberation. Reclaiming the Christian heritage of African Americans involves acknowledging that God is still on the side of the oppressed and working in and through humanity to bring about healing, restoration, freedom, and a renewed sense of hope and harmony within the African American community.[63] God must be lifted up not only as the Divine Liberator, but also as the One who comforts, sustains, and gives African Americans the ability to fight for their own liberation. Faith in God is not a passive faith that waits for God to work things out, but is an active faith that allows African Americans to make the necessary changes in their lives and in their communities.[64]

A renewed faith in God also involves knowing God personally, through Jesus Christ. As Melva Costen notes, a unique characteristic of African people is their belief that personal knowledge of God is paramount to knowing about God through doctrinal declarations, an approach that characterizes many Western-oriented Christians. Knowing God personally means experiencing the fullness of God through creation as well as through "God's revelational activity in one's own life and in the life of the community."[65]

Furthermore, a renewed faith in God acknowledges the liberating activity of Jesus Christ. This liberation is a holistic liberation that encompasses all aspects of human existence, including personal, spiritual, social, political, and economic concerns. According to James H. Harris, African American Christians believe that the liberating message of Jesus Christ "is one that is addressed to the despised and oppressed. He comforts and strengthens the weak, feeds the hungry, and heals the sick of their diseases — those who are on the 'underside of culture.'"[66] Harris further notes that the message of Christ is a message of hope for African Americans and poor people all over the world because it speaks directly to the present condition of those who are oppressed and suffering. For African Americans, Jesus is acknowledged as a "friend and advocate of the poor and oppressed."

Jesus is the Divine liberator who can bring about individual as well as communal transformation.[67]

African American churches that emphasize a renewed faith in God can provide a nurturing environment that will allow African Americans to encounter God in their own way, to deepen their relationship with God and others, and to discover the liberating activity of God through Jesus Christ in their own personal lives and in their communities.

The second Christian theme to be reclaimed is *reaffirming love*. In *Pastoral Theology: A Black-Church Perspective*, Harris asserts that the African American church has traditionally been concerned with instilling a positive sense of self-worth in African American people by teaching them that they are children of God, despite dehumanizing systems of oppression and discrimination.[68] Today, developing a positive self-esteem is still a crucial part of the ministry of the African American church. Building a positive self-esteem is essential, according to Harris, if the church and community are to "make a real difference in changing the conditions of our society."[69]

The Christian component of the triple-heritage can assist African Americans in developing a greater sense of self-esteem and self-worth by reaffirming love for self and others as human beings created in the image of God. In Genesis 1:27, the creation story affirms the uniqueness of every person and asserts the creation of each person in the image and likeness of God. In this respect, love goes beyond a sentimental feeling and involves a genuine respect, appreciation, and affirmation of every person as valuable and loveable. When African Americans love themselves as children of God, they will be able to love others and to work together for the good of all of humanity.

Cornel West builds upon this notion of love in his discussion of a love ethic, which is a significant aspect of his "politics of conversion." According to West, "Self-love and love of others are both modes toward increasing self-valuation and encouraging political resistance in one's community."[70] He goes on to illustrate how this love ethic plays out, in a practical fashion, on a local, state, and national level on behalf of those who are striving to build a sense of agency among themselves to rise above the confines of this society.[71]

By reaffirming love for self and others, African Americans can be empowered to be actively involved in their communities so that they can participate in the ongoing effort to bring about significant changes for the benefit of all. The church can aid African Americans in this endeavor by helping them to see themselves as agents of change.

The third Christian theme to be reclaimed is *returning service.* In *African American Christian Worship,* Costen notes that "one of the strongest forces in traditional African life that continues among African Americans is a deep sense of kinship or relatedness."[72] This relatedness encompasses all of creation, which is perceived as sacred and good in God's eyes. Given that the created order includes humanity, "human beings are to exist in unity with one another and with all of creation." This sense of oneness demonstrates a sense of community where all of creation works together to sustain life.[73] Costen goes on to suggest, "This understanding of community created by the kinship system is a reminder that individuals exist as a part of the corporate whole. One becomes aware of self, duties, privileges, and responsibilities in terms of others."[74] This sense of cooperation is exemplified in the African adage: "I am, because we are; and since we are, therefore I am."[75]

Returning service means participating as an active member of the community and giving back to the community that has helped to shape individual lives. Such service can be achieved through directed action. Directed action is defined, in this discussion, as action that is intentional, focused, and moving towards social, economic, political, spiritual, and physical change within society. It incorporates individual, communal, public, and private involvement of persons within as well as outside of the African American community. It also involves rethinking educational systems, mobilizing and redirecting African American dollars, tapping into available resources, reassessing current values and responsibilities, and developing a system of support that allows African Americans to do whatever is necessary to bring about practical changes within their communities.

An example of a support system within the community that can be incorporated as a part of a Christian outreach ministry is a mentoring program known as the Birthing Project. This program matches pregnant African American women who are at risk with other African American women who become their "sister friends" and walk with them throughout the entire pregnancy and up to one year after the baby is born. During this time, the women address issues of nutrition, contraception, health care for the baby and mother, family support systems, and the many other concerns that may arise during and after pregnancy. The program is designed to reduce the high infant mortality rate of African American babies. Programs such as this, which are developed through directed action, enable African Americans to provide valuable service by addressing the various needs that are currently present within the African American community. Moreover, directed action can strengthen a sense of kinship among all African Americans.

The Christian component of the triple-heritage enables African Americans to live out their Christian faith while celebrating their distinctiveness as African American Christians. Furthermore, by renewing faith, reaffirming love, and returning service, African Americans can rise above the unique challenges within the African American community and embrace a renewed sense of pride and dignity that allows them to live as valued and contributing members of society.

Implications for Christian Education in the African American Church

The components of the triple-heritage offer three important insights for teaching the triple-heritage in the African American church.

First, a triple-heritage model of Christian education must emphasize the importance of knowing history, especially as it relates to people of African descent. While the African component of the triple-heritage places its primary emphasis on African history, which is inclusive of all African people, the African American component lends itself not only to a broad understanding of African history, but also to a particular understanding of African American history, which includes the African American experience of slavery, racism, and oppression. In a similar fashion, the Christian component of the triple-heritage embraces the Christian faith tradition while valuing the distinctiveness of African American Christianity.

The triple-heritage challenges the church to provide a holistic educational ministry that seeks to address the needs of the whole person. A holistic approach to Christian education requires a threefold vision. It must seek to address the intellectual, social, spiritual, physical, and emotional concerns of the congregation. It must value the sociohistorical context of African American people, which includes their African heritage, African American heritage, and Christian heritage. And it must educate African Americans to grow in their faith and inspire them to apply their faith through active participation within the community.

Second, a triple-heritage model of Christian education must be culturally sensitive, encouraging African Americans to celebrate their unique culture and value the contributions of African and African American people. The triple-heritage, which embraces a culturally sensitive approach to Christian education, challenges the church to provide a positive and accurate presentation of African and African American culture, including the contributions that people of African descent have made to society.

A culturally sensitive triple-heritage approach to Christian education also challenges the church to address both the individual and communal needs of the congregation. In the African American church, this would involve reflection upon economic, social, political, and racial oppression and how these realities affect both the individual and the community. A triple-heritage model of Christian education should be designed to equip persons to analyze these systems of oppression critically, to develop strategies for addressing these systems, and to move African Americans towards social action and transformation. In short, the triple-heritage recognizes the need to empower African American people to engage in historical analysis, sociopolitical examination, and cultural critique. Thus, it requires an educational program that stresses a praxis approach to education.

Moreover, a culturally sensitive triple-heritage approach to Christian education challenges the church to draw upon the sources that naturally emerge from African and African American culture, such as music, dance, ritual, folklore, art, literature, and indigenous modes of worship. These sources can richly enhance the educational ministry by inspiring a sense of creativity, spontaneity, and imagination.

Third, a triple-heritage model of Christian education must encourage the African American church to stand in solidarity with persons of African descent in the struggle for liberation. The triple-heritage challenges the church to address this concern by promoting education for justice and liberation. Anne Wimberly's model of story-linking may facilitate this effort, particularly since her model explores themes of liberation, vocation, and decision making through the sharing of personal, biblical, and African American faith heritage stories.[76] This model may be broadened to incorporate not only the stories of African American heritage, but also the stories, art, literature, and other modes of cultural expression that emerge from African heritage as well.

Teaching the triple-heritage will allow African Americans to delve into the deep river of their African American Christian heritage. In so doing, they will be inspired to affirm and celebrate who they are as Africans, African Americans, and Christians. A creative and illuminating way to explore the triple-heritage on a deeper level is to focus on the history and role of the spirituals. Because the spirituals embody all three aspects of the triple-heritage, they can provide lenses through which to explore the African, African American, and Christian traditions in a balanced and holistic manner. Chapter 3 presents the spirituals as a viable source for exploring the triple-heritage and its potential for Christian education.

Notes

1. Ali AlAmin Mazrui also uses the term triple-heritage in his book entitled *The Africans: A Triple-Heritage*. Mazrui describes the triple-heritage as indigenous African traditions, Islamic culture, and Western civilization (21). Mazrui engages in a critical analysis of Africa and how the dynamics of the triple-heritage have influenced the present condition of the motherland. Although these elements have contributed to numerous struggles in Africa, they also offer hope for her future. See Ali AlAmin Mazrui, *The Africans: A Triple-Heritage* (Boston: Little, Brown, 1986). At the time of this publication Mazrui was research professor at the University of Jos at Nigeria, and professor of Political Science and Afro-American Studies at the University of Michigan, Ann Arbor. Molefi Kete Asante and Hailu Habtu critique Mazrui, charging that his analysis of Africa is largely Eurocentric. They agree that Mazrui's study would benefit from an Afrocentric orientation.

See Molefi Kete Asante, *Kemet, Afrocentricity and Knowledge* (Trenton, N.J.: Africa World Press, 1990), 114–17; Hailu Habtu, "The Fallacy of the 'Triple-Heritage' Thesis: A Critique," *Issue* 13 (1984): 26–29.

2. First Institutional Baptist Church, *AACTS Parent-Student Handbook* (Phoenix: First Institutional Baptist Church, 1996), 3.

3. First Institutional Baptist Church, *AACTS Ministry: "To God Be the Glory"* (Phoenix: New Day Video Productions, 1996), videocassette.

4. My use of the term "African American" is intended to be inclusive of the larger group of Africans in the Diaspora in the United States. The triple-heritage, therefore, recognizes the diverse group of Africans in the Diaspora as well as those from the Caribbean, Bermuda, Britain, and African countries who reside in the United States.

5. First Institutional Baptist Church, "AACTS 1996–97 Pre K–6th Grade Program: Introducing the 'New' Middle School Program, 7th–9th Grades," brochure, First Institutional Baptist Church, Phoenix, 1996.

6. Henry H. Mitchell, *Black Belief: Folk Beliefs of Blacks in America and West Africa* (New York: Harper & Row, 1975), 1.

7. Leonard E. Barrett, *Soul Force: African Heritage in Afro-American Religion* (Garden City, N.Y.: Anchor Books, 1974), 37–39; Albert J. Raboteau, *Slave Religion: The "Invisible Institution" in the Antebellum South* (New York: Oxford University Press, 1978), 9–10; John S. Mbiti, *African Religions and Philosophy* (New York: Frederick A. Praeger, 1969), 15–16, 48–57.

8. Raboteau, 9. For a broader discussion on the Supreme Being in African traditions see E. Bolaji Idowu, *Olodumare: God in Yoruba Belief* (London: Longmans, Green and Co., 1962), 18–47, 52; Marjorie R. Bogen, "The Interaction of Art and Religion in the Culture of the Yorubas," in *The Black Experience in Religion,* ed. C. Eric Lincoln (Garden City, N.Y.: Doubleday, Anchor Press, 1974), 300–301; Kofi Asare Opoku, "Aspects of Akan Worship," in *The Black Experience in Religion,* ed. C. Eric Lincoln (Garden City, N.Y.: Doubleday, Anchor Press, 1974), 286, 296–97; Percy Amaury Talbot, *The Peoples of Southern Nigeria,* 3 vols. (London: Oxford University Press, 1926), 2:40–43; For additional resources see also J. B. Danquah, *The Akan Doctrine of God* (1944; reprint, London: Class, 1968); Daryll Forde and G. I. Jones, *The Ibibio-Speaking Peoples of South-Eastern Nigeria* (London: Oxford University Press, 1950).

9. Mbiti, *African Religions and Philosophy,* 100–109; A. R. Radcliffe-Brown, introduction to *African Systems of Kinship and Marriage,* ed. A. R. Radcliffe-Brown and Daryll Forde (New York: Oxford University Press, 1950), 3–6, 39–43; Nsenga Warfield-Coppock, *Adolescent Rites of Passage,* vol. 1 of *Afrocentric Theory and Applications* (Washington, D.C.: Baobab Associates, 1990), 12–14; Michelene R. Malson, *Understanding Black Single Parent Families: Stresses and Strengths,* Work in Progress,

no. 25 (Wellesley, Mass.: Stone Center for Developmental Services and Studies, 1987), 2–3.

10. Paul Hill, *Coming of Age,* 40–41; Paul Hill, "Raising Male Children," *The Drum: National Rites of Passage Institute* 1, no. 2 (1994): 1, 4–5; Delitha L. Morrow, "Rites of Passage," *Upscale* (May 1993): 55–56.

11. A. Okechukwu Ogbonnaya, *On Communitarian Divinity: An African Interpretation of the Trinity* (New York: Paragon House, 1994), 10–11. See also Mbiti's discussion in *African Religions and Philosophy,* 106–9.

12. John Hope Franklin, *From Slavery to Freedom: A History of Negro Americans,* 5th ed. (New York: Alfred A. Knopf, 1980), 48–49; E. Franklin Frazier, *The Negro Church in America* (New York: Schocken Books, 1963), 2–3. See also E. Franklin Frazier, *The Negro in the United States,* rev. ed. (New York: Macmillan, 1957).

13. Gayraud S. Wilmore, *Black Religion and Black Radicalism: An Interpretation of the Religious History of Afro-American People,* 2nd ed. (Maryknoll, N.Y.: Orbis Books, 1983), 240.

14. Franklin, 48–49; Frazier, *Negro Church in America,* 2–3.

15. Kelly Miller Smith Institute Inc., "What Does it Mean to Be Black and Christian?" in *Black Theology: A Documentary History,* vol. 2: *1980–1992,* ed. James H. Cone and Gayraud S. Wilmore, 2nd ed. (Maryknoll, N.Y.: Orbis Books, 1993), 167.

16. *Webster's Third New International Dictionary,* 3rd ed., s.v. "white" and "black." Quoted in Kelly Miller Smith Institute, Inc., 167.

17. Delores Williams, *Sisters in the Wilderness: The Challenge of Womanist God-Talk* (Maryknoll, N.Y.: Orbis Books, 1993), 85.

18. I learned this chant as a child on the playground. Although this is the version that I learned growing up, there are numerous variations.

19. Barrett, *Soul Force,* 14–15; Melville J. Herskovits, *The Myth of the Negro Past* (Boston: Beacon Press, 1958), 1–2. It is also important to note that Herskovits's view of African survivals is in sharp contrast to E. Franklin Frazier and others who maintained that Africans were virtually stripped of their culture through the process of enslavement. For a discussion of Frazier's view see Frazier, *The Negro Church in America* and *The Negro in the United States.*

20. Sid Lemelle, *Pan-Africanism for Beginners* (New York: Writers and Readers Publishing, 1992), 11.

21. Lemelle, 16–17.

22. Lemelle, 19.

23. Molefi Kete Asante, *The Afrocentric Idea* (Philadelphia: Temple University Press, 1987), 6; Molefi Kete Asante, *Afrocentricity* (Trenton, N.J.: Africa World Press, 1988), 6.

24. Lemelle, 12–14. For a broader and more complex discussion on Pan-Africanism see Josiah U. Young III, "God's Path and Pan-Africa," in *Black*

Theology: A Documentary History, vol. 2: 1980–1992, ed. James H. Cone and Gayraud S. Wilmore, 2nd ed. (Maryknoll, N.Y.: Orbis Books, 1993); and William Edward Burghardt Du Bois, "Pan-Africa and New Racial Philosophy," in The Seventh Son: The Thought and Writings of W. E. B. Du Bois, ed. Julius Lester, vol. 2 (New York: Random House, 1971). For additional resources see also Tony Martin, The Pan-African Connection: From Slavery to Garvey and Beyond (Dover, Mass.: Majority Press, 1983); Josiah U. Young III, A Pan-African Theology: Providence and the Legacies of the Ancestors (Trenton, N.J.: Africa World Press, 1992); and Ronald W. Walters, Pan Africanism in the African Diaspora: An Analysis of Modern Afrocentric Political Movements (Detroit: Wayne State University Press, 1993).

25. Asante, Afrocentricity, ix.

26. Molefi Kete Asante, Malcolm X as Cultural Hero and Other Afrocentric Essays (Trenton, N.J.: Africa World Press, 1993), 99–100.

27. Asante, Malcolm X, 100–101, 114.

28. Leonard Barrett, "African Religions in the Americas," in The Black Experience in Religion, ed. C. Eric Lincoln (Garden City, N.Y.: Doubleday, Anchor Press, 1974), 316; Barrett, Soul Force, 57; Herskovits, 87; Franklin, 40–41.

29. Herskovits, 87–88; Barrett, "African Religions," 316; Franklin, 40–41; Dwight N. Hopkins, "Slave Theology in the 'Invisible Institution,' " in Cut Loose Your Stammering Tongue: Black Theology in the Slave Narratives, ed. Dwight N. Hopkins and George Cummings (Maryknoll, N.Y.: Orbis Books, 1991), 32–33.

30. Herskovits, 87–88.

31. Quoted in Franklin, 40–41.

32. Barrett, "African Religions," 316.

33. Hopkins, 36–43; Henry Mitchell, 119.

34. Henry Mitchell, 118–20.

35. Arna Bontemps, introduction to The Book of Negro Folklore, ed. Langston Hughes and Arna Bontemps (New York: Dodd, Mead, 1958), viii.

36. Bontemps, introduction to The Book of Negro Folklore, viii.

37. Bontemps, introduction to The Book of Negro Folklore, ix.

38. Levine, 370–72.

39. Levine, 403–4.

40. Julius Lester, Black Folktales (New York: Grove Press, 1969), 61.

41. Levine, 386–89.

42. Levine, 396.

43. First Institutional Baptist Church, "AACTS," brochure.

44. J. Alfred Smith, Men's Day Sermon preached at Friendship Baptist Church, Yorba Linda, Calif., April 27, 1997.

45. Costen, 36–37; Frazier, *The Negro Church in America*, 10–11; Eugene D. Genovese, *Roll Jordan Roll: The World the Slaves Made* (New York: Pantheon Books, 1974), 162; Levine, 59–60; Henry Mitchell, 9–11; Raboteau, 4–5; Wilmore, 3–4, 7, 26.

46. See chapter 5 for a broader discussion of these and other theological themes embodied in the spirituals.

47. Costen, 39–48, 105; Ella Mitchell, 99–105; Janice E. Hale, "The Transmission of Faith to Young African American Children," in *The Recovery of Black Presence: An Interdisciplinary Exploration*, ed. Randall C. Bailey and Jacquelyn Grant (Nashville: Abingdon Press, 1995), 201–5.

48. C. Eric Lincoln and Lawrence H. Mamiya, *The Black Church in the African American Experience* (Durham, N.C.: Duke University Press, 1990), 3–4.

49. James H. Cone, *A Black Theology of Liberation*, 20th Anniversary ed. (1970; reprint, Maryknoll, N.Y.: Orbis Books, 1994), 87–88; Hopkins, 29–32; Levine, 33–34; Lincoln and Mamiya, 4.

50. Lincoln and Mamiya, 4.

51. J. Wendell Mapson Jr., *The Ministry of Music in the Black Church* (Valley Forge, Pa.: Judson Press, 1984), 21, 43–44; Costen, 91, 93; Joseph V. Crockett, *Teaching Scripture from an African American Perspective* (Nashville: Discipleship Resources, 1990), 28–30.

52. Costen, 93.

53. Costen, 93.

54. Costen, 105.

55. Costen, 106–9.

56. William Edward Burghardt Du Bois, *The Souls of Black Folk* (1903; reprint, New York: Bantam Books, 1989), 135.

57. Du Bois, *Souls of Black Folk*, 133–35.

58. Olivia Pearl Stokes, "Black Theology: A Challenge to Religious Education," in *Religious Education and Theology*, ed. Norma H. Thompson (Birmingham, Ala.: Religious Education Press, 1982), 85. For further discussion on the central role of the African American church, see also Du Bois, *Souls of Black Folk*, 136–37; Lincoln and Mamiya, 7–8; Mapson, 19.

59. See Cheryl Townsend Gilkes, "The Black Church as a Therapeutic Community: Suggested Areas for Research into the Black Religious Experience," *Journal of the Interdenominational Theological* Center 7, no. 1 (Fall 1980): 31–32; Marsha Foster Boyd, "The African American Church as a Healing Community: Theological and Psychological Dimensions of Pastoral Care," *Journal of Theology* 95 (1991): 15, 22; Christine Y. Wiley, "A Ministry of Empowerment: A Holistic Model for Pastoral Counseling in the African American Community," *Journal of Pastoral Care* 45, no. 4 (Winter 1991): 356–58.

60. Stokes, "Black Theology," 85.

61. Olivia Pearl Stokes, "The Educational Role of Black Churches in the 70s and 80s" (Philadelphia: United Church Press, Joint Educational Development, 1973), 4. This is one of three monographs in the packet *New Roads to Faith*.

62. For example, African American spirituals that embody these themes include: "Lord, I Want to Be a Christian," "I Want Jesus to Walk with Me," "Mah God Is So High," "We Shall Overcome," "You Hear the Lambs a-Cryin'," "God Is a God," and "I'm a-Rolling." See *Songs of Zion* (Nashville: Abingdon Press, 1981), 76, 95, 105, 127, 128, 140, 150.

63. Cone, *Black Theology of Liberation*, 55–58, 60–61, 74; Delores Williams, 4–5.

64. Cone, *Black Theology of Liberation*, 64; James H. Harris, *Pastoral Theology: A Black-Church Perspective* (Minneapolis: Fortress Press, 1991), 3–5.

65. Costen, 20.

66. James Harris, *Pastoral Theology*, 24.

67. James Harris, *Pastoral Theology*, 26.

68. James Harris, *Pastoral Theology*, 115.

69. James Harris, *Pastoral Theology*, 129.

70. Cornel West, *Race Matters* (Boston: Beacon Press, 1993), 19.

71. West, 19–20.

72. Costen, 21.

73. Costen, 21.

74. Costen, 22.

75. Costen, 22.

76. See Anne S. Wimberly, *Soul Stories: African American Christian Education* (Nashville: Abingdon Press, 1994).

Three

I'm Gonna Sing

Exploring the Spirituals

In chapter 2, the triple-heritage is defined as African, African American, and Christian. I also examined the implications for Christian education in the African American church through the lenses of this multifaceted heritage. The purpose of this chapter is to explore the potential of the spirituals as a key to the development of a Christian education model that will fully embody the triple-heritage. This chapter, therefore, includes explorations into the nature and character of the spirituals and the cultural and historical factors that have shaped them.

Nature of the Spirituals

Although the exact date of origin for the spirituals has never been pinpointed, many believe they first began to emerge around 1750 to 1775.[1] Furthermore, just as citing a specific date of origin for the spirituals is difficult, providing a single definition of these songs is difficult also. Thus, they have been described in a variety of ways. One of the leading African American intellectuals of the nineteenth century, W. E. B. Du Bois, referred to the spirituals as "Sorrow Songs."[2] In his writings, he states that they "are the articulate message of the slave to the world." He adds, "They are the music of an unhappy people, of the children of disappointment; they tell of death and suffering and unvoiced longing toward a truer world, of misty wanderings and hidden ways."[3]

> Sometimes I feel like a motherless chile,
> Sometimes I feel like a motherless chile,

> Sometimes I feel like a motherless chile,
> A long ways from home, A long ways from home.

Despite the overwhelming despair, Du Bois recognizes the beauty of the spirituals, which ultimately affirm a strong conviction that life would one day be transformed. He concludes, "Through all the sorrow of the Sorrow Songs there breathes a hope — a faith in the ultimate justice of things."[4]

> Then I get down on my knees an' pray,
> Get down on my knees an' pray.

Zora Neale Hurston, on the other hand, an African American anthropologist and prolific writer from 1920 to 1950, offers another view. Rejecting Du Bois's idea that all of the spirituals are sorrow songs, she maintains that they encompass a variety of subjects from a "peeve at gossips to Death and Judgment."[5] The "real spirituals," according to Hurston, are not simply songs, but rather they are "unceasing variations around a theme."[6] The spirituals, then, explore various themes from a number of perspectives. Thus, they can be shaped and reshaped depending upon the situation or circumstances of the people "performing" these songs.

Hurston also argues that the spirituals are always in the process of creation, and that they are meant to be sung with a group rather than as a solo. She explains that a genuine presentation of the spirituals is not possible because most of them have been altered by composers and arrangers. She refers to these spirituals as "Neo-Spirituals."[7] Hurston claims, regarding the spirituals, that "the nearest thing to a description one can reach is that they are Negro religious songs, sung by a group, and a group bent on expression of feelings and not on sound effects."[8] For Hurston, the spirituals are the songs of the people emerging out of their unique experience of oppression. Thus, Hurston understands the spirituals — more broadly than Du Bois — as communal religious songs of feeling.

Adding another dimension to the spirituals, Maud Cuney Hare, an African American writer, lecturer, and concert pianist during the early twentieth century, suggests that the spirituals embody the dynamic faith of the enslaved community. This faith was deeply rooted in the lived experience of the people, rather than rigid belief systems and doctrinal propositions. The spirituals, grounded in African heritage, also preserved the "paganism of African 'spirit' songs" and revealed the transformation of these songs through Christianity as interpreted by the enslaved community. In short, the spirituals are "the musical expression of spiritual emotion created *by* the race and not *for it.*"[9]

Like Du Bois and Hurston, Hare emphasizes the depth of emotion and feeling that emerges from these songs as well as their communal nature. Hare builds upon Du Bois and Hurston by reaching back to African origins as the foundation of these songs, but she adds that they are also influenced by Christian doctrines.

In a similar fashion, Arthur C. Jones emphasizes African origins in his definition of the spirituals, giving particular attention to the ring shout celebration, an African dance custom that continued during slavery.[10] Jones recognizes the influence of the Bible, and he also points out that the heavy emphasis in these songs is on the biblical stories from the Old Testament. The influence of the Old Testament can be seen in the spiritual "Ezek'el Saw de Wheel," based on Ezekiel 1:4–28.

> Ezek'el saw de wheel
> 'Way up in de middle o' de air,
> Ezek'el saw de wheel
> 'Way in de middle o' de air.
> De big wheel run by faith,
> De little wheel run by de Grace o' God,
> A wheel in a wheel
> 'Way in de middle o' de air.

In *The Spirituals and the Blues,* James Cone refers to the spirituals as "The power of song in the struggle for black survival."[11] He maintains that the spirituals illustrate "the essence of black religion."[12] According to Cone, the spirituals are "historical songs" that reveal the struggle for freedom, survival, and identity within the enslaved community. They not only illuminate the struggle, but they are also a "joyful experience, a vibrant affirmation of life and its possibilities...."[13] Cone thus adds a dynamic dimension to his concept of the role and function of the spirituals by emphasizing that they are a cultural expression that continues to be essential for the identity and survival of African Americans. While Cone does not reject Du Bois's characterization of the spirituals as sorrow songs that speak of death and suffering, Cone builds upon that description by also affirming Hurston's view of multiple themes and by suggesting that the spirituals also celebrate life and all that it has to offer.[14]

The spirituals, then, may be defined from several perspectives. Emerging out of the brutal institution of slavery, Christian influences, and African culture, they incorporated a wide variety of themes and functions. Resistance to the demands of slavery, the identification of the slaves with the children of Israel, the pain and sorrow of daily existence within the system of slavery, the hope for freedom, the supernatural power of God, the unique bond with Jesus of Nazareth, the longing for a closer walk with God, the war against sin and evil, the reality of Satan, the slave owners' deceit and hypocrisy, hope for the future, love, grace, justice, mercy, judgment, death, and eternal life — all are encompassed in the wide spectrum of issues addressed by the spirituals.[15]

But the spirituals are not only defined by content. They also embody a style of singing (group/communal) and a depth of emotion. The spirituals, as Du Bois so eloquently concludes, are the creation of a people "weary at heart"; yet even in the midst of despair, they are "the most beautiful expression of human experience born this side [of] the seas."[16]

Characteristics

As these several definitions show, the spirituals are a complex phenomenon, and no one definition has provided comprehensive meaning for or insight into them. While the previous descriptions shed light on the spirituals, they provide only a partial view of these songs. In an effort to broaden these definitions, Wyatt T. Walker in *"Somebody's Calling My Name"* outlines several characteristics that he believes are fundamental traits of the spirituals.

1. *Deep Biblicism.* Many spirituals are heavily influenced by the Bible, especially by Old Testament imagery. Spirituals that do not have a specific biblical reference often tend to have biblical overtones

and implications. In some spirituals, specific biblical stories or scriptural references can easily be identified.[17] For example, the story of the victorious battle of the Israelite army, led by Joshua against the city of Jericho (Josh. 6:1–27), is the theme of the spiritual "Joshua Fit de Battle of Jericho."

> Joshua fit de battle of Jericho, Jericho, Jericho;
> Joshua fit de battle of Jericho, an' de walls came tumblin' down.

2. *Eternality of Message.* Although the spirituals were created long ago, the message of many of these songs is both universal and contemporary. In other words, the message of numerous spirituals has transcended time and continues to speak to the human condition even today.[18] This transcendent quality is reflected in the spiritual "God Is a God."

> God is a God! God don't never change!
> God is a God an' He always will be God!

3. *Rhythm.* One of the strongest characteristics of the spirituals is rhythm. This aspect of the spirituals illustrates a strong link to Africa, where rhythm is a major part of the musical culture. The spirituals as genre or song are not limited to one particular rhythm. The rhythm may be "slow and plaintive," "driving and pulsating," rigorous and jubilant.[19] An example of a spiritual that can be sung with either a slow and contemplative rhythm or an upbeat and lively rhythm is "This Little Light of Mine."

> This little light of mine, I'm goin' to let it shine.
> Let it shine, let it shine, let it shine.[20]

4. *Improvisation.* Because the spirituals are flexible and spontaneous, they can be easily improvised to correspond or respond to changing events or situations.[21] One example is the spiritual entitled "Don' Let Nobody Turn You Aroun'," which was adapted and used during the civil rights movement in the 1960s, as discussed previously. An earlier version of the song was as follows:

> Don' let nobody turn you roun', turn you roun', turn you roun'.
> Don' let nobody turn you roun' walking up the King's Highway.

During the civil rights movement, it became:

> Don' let segregation turn you roun'...[22]

5. *Antiphony, or Call-and-Response.* Because this characteristic is commonly seen in African music, its presence in the spirituals is "strong evidence of an African survival in the New World."[23] It usually begins with a chant, sung by a leader or soloist who is followed by the group or congregation. This characteristic also illustrates the communal nature of the spirituals. The spiritual "Swing Low, Sweet Chariot" is an example.

> Leader: Swing low, sweet chariot,
> Response: Coming for to carry me home:
> Leader: Swing low, sweet chariot,
> Response: Coming for to carry me home.

6. *Double or Coded Meaning.* Some spirituals possess a dual or hidden meaning that allowed the slaves to communicate secret messages with one another without being detected by their masters. As described earlier, this feature can also be traced back to African practices of masking with symbols and double meanings.[24] Through their songs, Africans often related words of wisdom, insult, history, and humor with more than one meaning. While the spiritual "Steal Away" may have announced a secret meeting or an impending escape, the spiritual "Go Down, Moses" reflected the slaves' strong identification with the oppression of the children of Israel and communicated their belief in a God who identified with their suffering and would one day liberate them.

> When Israel was in Egypt's land: Let my people go;
> Oppressed so hard they could not stand, Let my people go.
> Go down, Moses, 'Way down in Egypt land,
> Tell ole Pharaoh, Let my people go.

7. *Repetition.* Many spirituals repeat the melody, lyrics, or both with minimal changes throughout the song. Repetition, also of African influence, helped to facilitate a corporate memory and contemporary significance.[25] The spiritual entitled "Were You There?" illustrates this characteristic.

> Were you there when they crucified my Lord?
> Were you there when they crucified my Lord?
> Oh! Sometimes it causes me to tremble, tremble, tremble.
> Were you there when they crucified my Lord?

8. *Unique Imagery.* Many spirituals such as "Were You There?" create powerful imagery.[26] The images created by these songs are often so dynamic and vivid that one can actually visualize or feel the images portrayed. This unique quality is also illustrated by the spiritual "Hush, Hush, Somebody's Callin' Mah Name."

> Hush. Hush. Somebody's callin' mah name.
> Hush. Hush. Somebody's callin' mah name,
> Oh mah Lawd, Oh mah Lawdie, what shall I do?
> Sounds like Jesus. Somebody's callin' mah name.
> Sounds like Jesus. Somebody's callin' mah name,
> Oh mah Lawd, Oh mah Lawdie, what shall I do?
> Soon one mornin', death'll come creepin' in mah room,
> Soon one mornin', death'll come creepin' in mah room.
> Oh mah Lawd, Oh mah Lawdie, what shall I do?

Walker's contribution of these eight characteristics suggests that the spirituals embody various themes and styles arising from particular cultural influences. He illustrates this point in the chart on the following page, which provides a general comparison of the basic characteristics of African music and the slave spirituals.[27]

Taken with other definitions, then, the spirituals could be defined as the form of music arising from the unique convergence of African culture, slave experience, and Christian religion. In other words, the spirituals embody the triple-heritage.

COMPARISON CHART

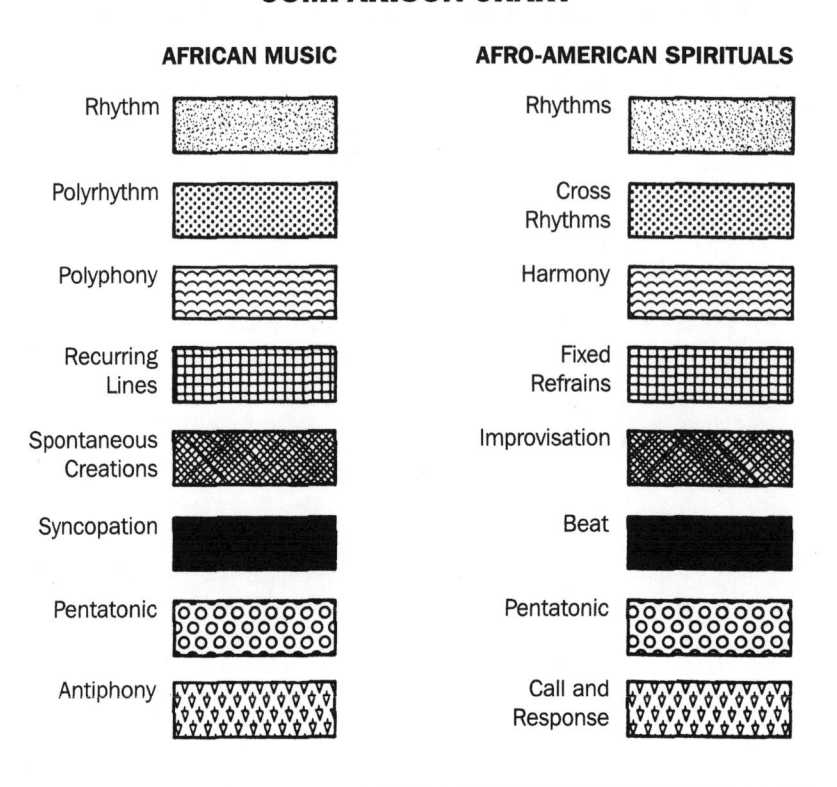

AFRICAN MUSIC	AFRO-AMERICAN SPIRITUALS
Rhythm	Rhythms
Polyrhythm	Cross Rhythms
Polyphony	Harmony
Recurring Lines	Fixed Refrains
Spontaneous Creations	Improvisation
Syncopation	Beat
Pentatonic	Pentatonic
Antiphony	Call and Response

Historical Background

A more careful analysis of the African, African American, and Christian influences that shaped the spirituals is divided here into discussions of their African roots, the development of the spirituals, and slave religion.

African Roots: Worldview

The Africans who came to America as slaves arrived in the New World deeply rooted in a rich heritage, a dynamic worldview, and the wisdom of their ancestors. African American culture was thus significantly shaped by the African culture that was brought to this country and passed on to subsequent generations.[28] This process took place as Africans from numerous tribal backgrounds arrived in this country and began to incorporate various aspects of the new world into their cosmology.[29] These cosmologies "found expression in the spirituals, music, dance, and the general life-style of later generations who came to be known as Afro-Americans."[30]

The African worldview that shaped the life, understanding, and cultural expression of the slaves emphasized the connectedness and harmonious relationships among all living things including God, humanity, nature, and various forms of spiritual beings. Inanimate objects were also valued in that they were created to meet the needs of human beings.[31] This type of connectedness is grounded in a strong sense of community, which forms the basis of the African worldview. According to Ogbonnaya, "Communality, relationality, and fundamental interconnectedness" are vital to the African understanding of "seeing and being in the world." Furthermore, intentional efforts to build and maintain community by working together in harmony are held in highest esteem.[32] Thus this unifying nature of the African worldview creates a spiritual tie among people forming a "communal bond that is unbreakable by distance or death."[33]

Because all are connected for the African, all aspects of life are highly valued and considered sacred. Africans accordingly strive to live life to the fullest by respecting the harmonious balance between God, humanity, and nature. These elements, according to Levine, are "distinct but inseparable aspects of a sacred whole."[34] Similarly, because all of creation emerges from the Supreme Being, and because Africans understand everything as sacred, we can conclude that in traditional African thought nothing was perceived as "totally profane."[35]

The connectedness and sacredness of all things leads, in turn, to an affirmation of life, which compels Africans to participate fully in the whole of life. This aspect of the African worldview can be seen in African music, dance, folklore, storytelling, and proverbs. Through these modes of expression, Africans share their beliefs and feelings; rehearse their history; critique the establishment; set forth their worldview; observe rituals and ceremonies; communicate with others within the community; govern their moral behavior in relationship to God, humanity, and creation; impart wisdom for full participation in life; and provide guidelines for instruction.[36] An

African worldview thus embodies a sense of connectedness, unity, sacredness, and life.

African traditional religion,[37] which is grounded in this worldview, is deeply concerned with the success of the community. For instance, Africans place great emphasis on communal cooperation. Thus, meaningful interpersonal interactions within the community are vital because they allow individuals to embrace the fullness of their humanity. For Africans, the nature of community includes both "the freedom of the individual within the community, and the responsibility of the individual for the community."[38] To this end, Africans respect the relationship between humanity and the spiritual realm, particularly given that their conception of community includes the living, the dead, and often the unborn.[39] Of course, African traditional religion is more complex than merely a concern for community. Margaret Creel adds that it includes a belief in the Supreme Deity, belief in the continuation of life beyond death, respect for the ancestors, and belief in the "Supernatural causation of suffering, disease, accidents [and] death," for which "Magic and medicine were employed."[40]

For many Africans who were brought to the new world, religion was the central aspect of their being. As Jessie Mulira states:

> Religion was (and remains) a vital part of the lives of most Africans. For some it encompassed their entire existence. It substantiated and explained their place in the universe, their culture, and their relationship to nature and humankind; it also dictated their roles in the community and society at large. Religion among most African ethnic groups was not simply a faith or worship system; it was a way of life, a system of social control, a provider of medicine, and an organizing mechanism.[41]

Thus, many Africans held religion in high esteem, for it was an integral part of their total being and it permeated every aspect of their lives. Not surprisingly, then, the music of the enslaved African community was intensely religious.

African Roots: Music in the Tradition

In Africa, music is a vital part of the rituals and traditions of the people. In fact, almost every aspect of African life is accompanied by music. For example, music is used when the African is "born, named, initiated into manhood, warriored, armed, housed, betrothed, wedded, [and] buried."[42] Music is also used in work, play, leisure, and artistic expression. In essence, music permeates every aspect of human life, and its expression brings about fellowship, unity, and celebration.

Singing, dancing, and instruments are all important components of African music. Although Africans employ a variety of instruments including xylophones, rattles, horns, calabashes, trumpets, stringed instruments, and flutes, the drum is without a doubt the instrument of choice. Drums, in various sizes and shapes, function in numerous ways including accompaniment for dancing and singing as well as communication throughout the community.[43] Dance similarly accompanies music at the forefront of significant life celebrations such as births, deaths, baptisms, and marriages. It further functions, however, as a facilitator of communal involvement, a means of creative and political expression, and a viable mode of education. Also critical to African music is singing, which is both communal and universal.[44]

African songs are often spontaneous, "full of emphatic gusto," antiphonal, improvisational, free, celebrative, unmeasured, rhythmic, and responsorial. Other characteristics include: call-and-response, recurrent incremental lines, repetition, short phrases, syncopation, and various themes reflecting on life, the universe, nature, and politics.[45] As Lovell observes, "All these characteristics, unique to or emphatic in Africa, appear over and over in the spiritual."[46]

African Roots: Influence on the Spirituals

Although many years and many miles have separated Africans and African Americans, evidence of their common heritage can still be seen in their religious expression. The strongest connection between the African and African American religious expression is their common belief in a Supreme Being, who is the creator and sustainer of the universe and is not limited to time and space. Because the cosmos, in the mind of Africans, is considered sacred, everything reflects "the sacred nature of the cosmos," including the whole of their cultural expression.[47] Hence, the slaves were able to convey their religious beliefs at any time through various circumstances regardless of their location. This orientation was vital, according to Paris, because it "enabled African peoples on the continent and in the diaspora to live in the presence of their gods and to view all things as ordered or disordered by the latter's will."[48] The spirituals reflect these aspects of the African worldview and traditional African religious beliefs as well. For example, the sacred nature of reality, the belief in a Supreme Being, and the holistic integration of all aspects of the world can be seen in the spiritual "He's Got the Whole World in His Hands."

> He's got the whole world in His hands,
> He's got the big, round world in His hands,
> He's got the whole world in His hands,
> He's got the whole world in His hands.

The verses go on to acknowledge that God has "the wind and the rain," "the sun and the moon," "the little bitty baby," "brothers and sisters," and "everybody" in God's hands. Although not much is known about the origin of this song, some believe that it was a praise song for God, the creator and sustainer of the universe, which emerged through the oral tradition and expressed the slaves' belief that God's power undergirded and directed all of life regardless of the situation.[49] The slaves believed that the whole world was guided and controlled by a Supreme Being — God. Because God was in control, they knew that God was concerned about every aspect of the world. God was also intimate and loving and held every person in God's hands. Thus, in God, all people were embraced as family members, kinfolks, and sisters and brothers surrounded by God's love. Therefore, the slaves were convinced that God would ultimately overcome their peculiar situation. God was in control, not the forces of oppression. Thus, their unwavering belief in an all-powerful God gave them the ability to endure the brutality of slavery. Many other spirituals also incorporate this notion of the sacredness and value of all aspects of the world.

The African influence can also be seen in the creative way that the African slaves drew upon their understanding of the world to develop not only a new community and a new religion, but also an elaborate system of survival, protection, power, and control based on the African practice of coding. This practice was traditionally performed in an open forum where Africans were at liberty to express their

Exploring the Spirituals

thoughts and sentiments concerning their leaders as well as others within the community through music, dance, metaphor, and other modes of artistic expression.[50] In an effort to exercise some sense of power and control within their situation, the slave community similarly incorporated coded messages in many of the spirituals to "conceal their business from the overseers and the plantation owners."[51] Sometimes these messages announced a secret meeting: "Walk together, children, Don't you get weary, There's a great camp-meeting in the Promised Land." Others may have signaled an impending escape: "Steal away, steal away, steal away to Jesus! Steal away, steal away home, I ain't got long to stay here!" Still others were used to mock their masters and to expose their religious hypocrisy: "Heav'n, heav'n, Ev'rybody talkin' 'bout heav'n ain't goin' there, Heav'n, heav'n, Goin' to shout all over God's heav'n." Thus, the practice of coding can be seen in numerous spirituals.

Another aspect of African heritage that is reflected in the spirituals is the high regard for religion. During the time of slavery, many slaves continued to value religion very highly, as the following spiritual illustrates:

> O walk Jordan long road,
> And religion so sweet;
> O religion is good for anything,
> And religion so sweet.
> Religion make you happy.
> Religion gib me patience.
> O member, get religion.
> I long time been a-huntin'.
> I seekin' for my fortune.
> O I gwine to meet my Savior.
> Gwine to tell him 'bout my trials....

Just as religion was a vital part of the life and existence of most Africans, many slaves continued to embrace religion as the central focus of their lives. Through religion the enslaved community struggled to make sense of their peculiar situation, to gain some sense of power and control, and to find healing in the midst of their deepest despair.

But more than just African themes can be seen in the spirituals; the unique characteristics of African music are reflected as well. Just as music is an integral part of the customs and practices of African people, accompanying all aspects of life, so it was also pervasive in the slave community (a point that is elaborated upon below). Characteristics such as repetition and call-and-response are present in both African music and the spirituals. James Weldon Johnson notes that the structure of the spirituals is often identical to that of African music. For example, both incorporate recurrent incremental leading lines with a repeating choral response. Drawing upon Denham and Clapperton's *Narrative of Travels in Northern and Central Africa,* Johnson cites the following song by the people of Bornou.

> Give flesh to the hyenas at daybreak—
> Oh, the broad spears!
> The spear of the Sultan is the broadest—
> Oh, the broad spears!
> I behold thee now, I desire to see none other—
> Oh, the broad spears!...[52]

Another African song illustrating the same characteristics is taken from a Bantu folktale entitled *The Story of Tangalimlibo.*

> It is crying, it is crying,
> Sihamba Ngenyanga.
> The child of the walker by moonlight,
> Sihamba Ngenyanga.
> It was done intentionally by people, whose names cannot be mentioned
> Sihamba Ngenyanga.
> They sent her for water during the day,
> Sihamba Ngenyanga...[53]

When these African songs are compared to the African American spiritual "Oh, Wasn't Dat a Wide Ribber," the similarities are striking.

> Oh, de Ribber of Jordan is deep and wide,
> One mo' ribber to cross.

> I don't know how to get on de other side,
> One mo' ribber to cross.
> Oh, you got Jesus, hold him fast,
> One mo' ribber to cross.
> Oh, better love was nebber told,
> One mo' ribber to cross.... [54]

Finally, the communal nature of African music is also reflected by the use of music in the slave community. As in Africa, music was primarily sung in and for the community. Hence music also became an integral part of the enslaved community in America. Affirming that they were gonna sing regardless of their circumstances, the slaves sang as the Spirit moved them in affirmation of life and its many joys, challenges, and transitions. The spirituals, then, emerged through this new community, which fostered a unique setting for critical, reflective, and creative expression.

As African slaves began to adjust to life in the new world, they embraced a number of beliefs and practices that allowed them to shape a viable community and to survive under the brutal system of chattel slavery. Levine writes, "it was in the spirituals that slaves found a medium which resembled in many crucial ways the cosmology they had brought with them from Africa and afforded them the possibility of both adapting to and transcending their situation."[55] Though the enslaved community was transformed over the years, the spirituals continued to spring forth with a universal message of hope and inspiration that transcended cultural, geographical, and political boundaries.

The spirituals therefore embody critical aspects of African heritage. These can be discerned in the expansive worldview and religious perspective of the spirituals, their communal emphasis, their use of rhythm and coded messages, and their adaptive nature.

Development of the Spirituals

Though the spirituals first appeared after 1750, no organized effort to collect them was made until after the Civil War when Charlotte Forten and Thomas Wentworth Higginson recorded some of the songs that they had heard. In 1867, William F. Allen, Charles P.

Ware, and Lucy McKim Garrison were the first to formally compile a substantive collection of the spirituals.[56]

The popularity of the spirituals increased in 1871 when the Fisk University Jubilee Singers began presenting the spirituals in concert in the United States and abroad. Other black institutions and individual artists also began to arrange, compose, and feature the spirituals in their own performances. Although the spirituals have been shaped and reshaped over the years and often no longer resemble their original form, they continue to evoke a sense of passion and hope whenever they are performed. The spirituals continue to serve as a source of inspiration for many people throughout the world.[57]

Before their more general popularity, of course, the spirituals had played a vital role in the life of the slaves and particularly in their religious life. The poignant and powerful accounts of numerous slaves, whether bound or free, indicate that the slaves placed great value on their private worship services.

Although some slaves often worshiped in the presence of their masters or overseers, they preferred to have their own private services so that they could worship as they pleased. While some slaves were allowed, and even encouraged, to attend religious services, usually conducted by white preachers, many were not permitted to attend any type of religious gathering. They risked harsh punishment and even death if they were caught attending services of any kind. Their determination to worship in their own way prevailed, however, and even in the midst of great peril they found a way to attend these secret religious services.[58] These clandestine services, the "invisible institution," were held in the slave quarters or in secluded areas known as "hush harbors" or "bush arbors."

The invisible institution became a primary locus for the development of the spirituals. For one thing, they were part of an elaborate system developed to conceal the meetings. Messages encoded in the spirituals could communicate the time and place of the next meeting. Another interesting aspect of the slaves' system of secrecy was the use of an iron kettle, turned upside down in the middle of the group to catch the sound during their secret worship services. As an ex-slave reflected, "All the noise would go into that kettle; They could shout and sing all they wanted to and the noise wouldn't go outside."[59]

As Raboteau points out, it is difficult to determine whether these kettles operated symbolically or played a practical role in reducing the sound. This would be interesting to know, especially since these secret services were lively, loud, and festive celebrations that usually consisted of prayer, praise, singing, dancing, shouting, preaching, and fellowship.[60] Some have suggested, however, that the use of the pots by the slaves may have been "a remnant of African custom."[61]

The spirituals were an integral part of these worship services. The slaves spontaneously created songs during the services, where they served as praise songs that expressed their love, adoration, and confidence in God as well as corporate prayers that voiced their cares and concerns. Spirituals were also important educational tools that taught worshipers about the Bible, God, Jesus, sin, Satan, and communal ethics as well as personal and collective empowerment.

The spirituals were not only a vital part of the invisible institution, but they also served an important function in the work environment of the slaves. Most of the slaves in the United States lived on southern plantations in the early years of the nineteenth century. These plantations produced vast quantities of rice and cotton. Slaves, whether working in the plantation house or in the field, were expected to put in long hours of backbreaking work, with a minimal amount of food and rest. To keep up with this pace, the slaves often sang as they worked, using music just as it had been used in Africa.[62] Music was thus a central part of their daily work routine, whether "picking cotton, threshing rice, stripping tobacco, harvesting sugar cane, or doing the endless small jobs on the plantation."[63] As one ex-slave reflected, "We would pick cotton and sing, pick and sing all day."[64]

Many spirituals originated in the work context. Of the many types of work songs, three in particular seem to emerge most often. First were songs used for work where no "rhythmic movement" was involved. In this case, a recurring line may have been repeated as the slaves completed their work.[65] The song "John Henry," based on the legendary hero, illustrates:

> This ol' hammer killed John Henry!
> This ol' hammer killed John Henry!

> This ol' hammer killed John Henry,
> But this ol' hammer won't kill me![66]

Another type of work song reflects the interaction among the workers, their work, and their overseers. The song "Captain, O Captain" reflects this theme.[67]

> Captain, O captain, you must be cross,
> It's six o'clock an' you won't "knock-off!"
> Captain, O captain you must be blin'
> You keep hollerin' "hurry" an' I'm darn nigh flyin'.[68]

Finally, rhythmic songs were used for work involving systematic or uniform movement by the workers and were often used to set and keep the pace of the work.[69] The song "Raise the Iron" illustrates the ability of the leader and the workers to "pull together" in a cooperative effort to complete their work.[70]

> Brother Rabbit, Brother Bear, Can't you line them just a hair?
> Shake the iron, um-uh! Down the railroad, um-uh!
> Well, raise the iron, um-uh! Raise the iron, um-uh!
> Well, is you got it, um-uh! Well, raise the iron, um-uh!
> Raise the iron, um-uh! Throw the iron, um-uh!
> Throw the iron — throw it away!

The spirituals also provided a means of expressing the hope and despair that arose out of the living conditions under the brutal system of chattel slavery. Slaves were considered property and bought and sold at the whim of the white slaveholders. Under this system, families were torn apart, women were raped, and children were forced to work at an early age. Slaves who were unable to complete their assigned duties for the day were often subjected to brutal punishment. Slaves had no rights, so slave masters were rarely prosecuted if a slave was killed in the course of his or her punishment.[71] The slaves sang about the anguish and despair that was often a part of their daily existence: "Nobody knows the trouble I see, Nobody knows my sorrow; Nobody knows the trouble I see, Glory, hallelujah!" In the midst of such hardships, the spirituals emerged as a source of strength, support, encouragement, survival, hope, and freedom.

On a deeper level, the spirituals and other songs created by the enslaved community served the dual purpose of not only preserving communal values and solidarity but also providing occasions for the individual to transcend, at least symbolically, the inevitable restrictions of environment and society by permitting an expression of deeply held feelings that ordinarily could not be verbalized.[72]

The importance of the spirituals and other songs produced by the enslaved community did not end with the abolition of slavery. They continue to influence American culture even today. For instance, the spirituals and work songs have significantly affected the development of other types of music, including "minstrel songs, jazz, blues, country music, popular songs, ring-game songs, swing, White rock, 'soul' music, and gospel music."[73] These songs have not only shaped the world of music, but they have also profoundly influenced other forms of artistic expression such as dance, drama, literature, and art.[74]

The spirituals themselves have been resurrected in recent times in the civil rights movement. For example, the spiritual "Woke Up This Morning with My Mind Stayed on Jesus" was changed to "Woke Up This Morning with My Mind Stayed on Freedom," and the text of C. A. Tindley's hymn "I'll Overcome Someday" was merged with the spiritual tune "I'll Be Alright" to create the theme song of the civil rights movement, "We Shall Overcome."[75] Thus, during the height of this movement, freedom songs, often derived from spirituals, served as vital sources of community pride, inspiration, purpose, solidarity, unity, encouragement, and support.

Slave Religion

The spirituals not only reflect African and African American heritage, but they also reflect the encounter of the enslaved community with the Christian heritage.

In *Deep River and the Negro Spiritual Speaks of Life and Death,* Howard Thurman suggests that the spirituals reflect the religion of the enslaved community by drawing upon three main sources: the "Bible" (i.e., the "slave canon"), nature, and the slaves' religious experience. According to Thurman, the stories and images drawn from the Bible appear to favor the Old Testament. Because the slaves were able to identify readily with the plight of the Hebrew children of God, they immediately internalized their story of bondage and liberation. "Go Down, Moses" and "Didn't My Lord Deliver Daniel?" are two examples of spirituals that are drawn from the Old Testament.[76]

The New Testament also served as a rich resource for the spirituals, many of which reflect substantial interest in the life and death of Jesus Christ. The majority of spirituals explicitly influenced by the New Testament suggest that the slaves more readily identified with the suffering, death, and resurrection of Jesus than with his birth.[77] Thus, the enslaved community was able to interweave their own experience of suffering with the story of the crucifixion.[78] The spiritual "He Nevuh Said a Mumbalin' Word" illustrates:

> They crucified my Lord,
> An' He nevuh said a mumbalin' word,
> They crucified my Lord,
> An' He nevuh said a mumbalin' word,
> Not a word, not a word, not a word.

Other spirituals, such as "Were You There?" and "Calvary," also reflect their identification with the suffering of Jesus.

The slaves, however, did not see Jesus as one who was defeated. Rather, in the resurrection, they saw him as conquering king and liberator, and they firmly believed that he would one day deliver them from the bonds of slavery.

> He's King of Kings, and Lord of Lords,
> Jesus Christ, the first and last,
> No man works like him.
> He built a platform in the air,
> No man works like him.
> He meets the saints from everywhere,
> No man works like him.
> He pitched a tent on Canaan's ground.
> No man works like him.
> And broke the Roman Kingdom down,
> No man works like him.[79]

However, the birth theme also appears occasionally and powerfully in the spirituals, as "Go, Tell It on the Mountain" illustrates:

> Go, tell it on the mountain,
> Over the hills and everywhere,
> Go, tell it on the mountain
> That Jesus Christ is born.[80]

Other spirituals containing birth themes include "Mary Had a Baby," "Sister Mary Had-a But One Child," "Three Wise Men to Jerusalem Came," and "Lit'l Boy, How Ole Are You?"

In addition to the Bible or the "slave canon," the ideas that emerged out of the world of nature also provided a wealth of constructive content for the spirituals. These nature songs were usually very basic and drew insights and comparisons between various aspects of nature and the slaves' existence. For instance, the slaves' observation of and creative identification with the inchworm can be seen in the spiritual "Keep a-Inchin' Along."

> Keep a inchin' along,
> Massa Jesus comin' by an' by,
> Keep a inchin' along like a po' inchworm,
> Massa Jesus comin' by an' by.[81]

The spirituals were also influenced by the personal and communal religious experiences of the slaves. This source served as a means of religious expression through which the slaves revealed both the challenges and the victories of their faith journey. Inspired by the words of the psalmist, "Let the redeemed of the Lord say so," in Psalm 107:2, the slaves testified to their faith in the spiritual "Certainly, Lord."[82]

> Have you got good religion?
> Cert'nly, Lord! ...
> Have you been redeemed?
> Cert'nly, Lord! ...
> Have you been to the water?
> Cert'nly, Lord! ...

> Have you been baptized?
> Cert'nly, Lord!...
> Cert'nly, Cert'nly, Cert'nly, Lord!

The slaves wanted to live a life that reflected their faithfulness to God, especially in light of the religious hypocrisy of the slaveholders. This longing for faithfulness inspired them to sing,

> Lord, I want to be a Christian in my heart,...
> Lord, I want to be more loving in my heart,...
> Lord, I want to be more holy in my heart,...
> Lord, I want to be like Jesus in my heart,...

The religious experiences of the slaves served not only as a means of religious expression, but also as a vehicle for the slaves to express their inner emotions and deepest longings. Because the slaves saw themselves as children of God and understood that they were created by God to be free, they often expressed their desire for freedom through the spirituals. Thurman indicates, "Freedom from slavery and freedom from life were often synonymous."[83] Many times the desire for freedom through death became the dominant focus; however, this desire did not mean that the slaves had accepted the constraints of slavery. The tone of many spirituals indicates that some of the slaves were determined to resist in this world.[84] This spirit of resistance is expressed in several lines of the spiritual "O Freedom":

> An' befo' I'd be a slave,
> I'll be buried in my grave,
> An' go home to my Lord an' be free.

This profound and courageous expression of the Christian faith was unambiguous in its call for both spiritual and physical liberation.

Drawing from stories of the Bible, the slaves' physical surroundings, and their own personal religious experiences, the spirituals were thus fashioned as a unique means of providing hope and sustaining faith in the midst of the brutalities of slavery.

The Spirituals as a Source for Enhancing the Educational Ministry in the African American Church

Given that the spirituals clearly embody all three aspects of the triple-heritage, we must now consider how they might be used as an effective method of teaching Christian education within the African American community (and perhaps the wider community as well).

In his article "An African-American Method of Religious Education," Joseph Crockett identifies three assumptions that undergird effective methods of Christian education from an African American perspective. First, the African American experience must be the context out of which the methods arise. Second, the methods must reject the generalizing assumptions of "universality" and also the limitations of a narrow historical or "cultural specificity." Thus, while addressing the specific concerns of the African American community, the methods should also lend themselves to informed use by persons from other cultures. Third, African American Christian educators must play an active role in designing educational programs that uncompromisingly address the needs of the African American community while also addressing important concerns of the wider community. Designing such programs requires educators to work in partnership with recipients of these programs to develop the most effective programs for their communities.[85]

The use of the spirituals could be an effective method of Christian education, according to Crockett's criteria. Concerning his first point, the spirituals are an integral part of the African American culture because they were born out of the African American experience of slavery, and they include a holistic view of African American Christian heritage that embraces African roots, African American history, and the Christian faith. Because the spirituals embody all three aspects of this heritage, they can be an effective way to explore the heritage and to guide a process of education that is communal, emotive, praxis oriented, critical, and tradition bearing, yet future directed and creative.

Use of the spirituals can further address Crockett's final two criteria in that they possess a unique yet universal message that continues to resonate across generational and cultural borders. Although the spirituals were created many years ago, they continue to influence not only the African American community, but the wider society as well. This influence makes possible the creation by Christian educators of a paradigm of Christian education that speaks inside the African American community and beyond. People within the African American community can continue to sing the wisdom of the spirituals, while people from other cultures can experience the spirituals as a source of inspiration and as a vehicle for exploring both their own and the African American heritage. Working together, we can all sing when the Spirit says a-Sing.

In this chapter, then, we have seen that the spirituals both embody the triple-heritage and may be foundational in developing a more expansive model of Christian education. The various theological foundations and implications of this new model of Christian education are explored in the next chapter.

Notes

1. Mark P. Bangert, "Black Gospel and Spirituals: A Primer," *Currents in Theology and Mission* 16, no. 3 (1989): 174; William Farley Smith, "Cries of Freedom in Afro-American Spirituals: Music/Worship Aids for Martin Luther King, Jr. Birthday Celebration and Black History Recognition," *Drew Gateway* 61, no. 1 (1991): 60–71; Wyatt Walker, 40; Lovell, 63; John W. Work, ed., *American Negro Songs and Spirituals* (New York: Bonanza Books, 1940), 1. For other perspectives on the origin of the spirituals see also Fisher, *Negro Slave Songs;* Eileen Southern, *The Music of Black Americans: A History* (New York: W. W. Norton, 1971); Dena J. Epstein, *Sinful Tunes and Spirituals: Black Folk Music to the Civil War,* Music in American Life (Urbana: University of Illinois Press, 1977); Dena J. Epstein, "A White Origin for the Black Spirituals? An Invalid Theory and How It Grew," *American Music* 1, no. 2 (1983): 53–59; and Arnold Shaw, *Black Popular Music in America: From the Spirituals, Minstrels, and Ragtime to Soul, Disco, and Hip-Hop* (New York: Schirmer Books, 1986).

2. Du Bois, *Souls of Black Folk,* 177.
3. Du Bois, *Souls of Black Folk,* 179–80.
4. Du Bois, *Souls of Black Folk,* 186.
5. Hurston, 15.
6. Hurston, 15.
7. Hurston, 15.

8. Hurston, 15.
9. Hare, 21.
10. Arthur C. Jones, *Wade in the Water: The Wisdom of the Spirituals* (Maryknoll, N.Y. Orbis Books, 1993), 6. See chapter 6 below for a description of this custom.
11. Cone, *Spirituals and the Blues*, 1.
12. Cone, *Spirituals and the Blues*, 29.
13. Cone, *Spirituals and the Blues*, 29–31.
14. The spirituals have also been described by others with terms like slave songs, jubilees, Negro Spirituals, folk songs, work songs, shuffles, ring spirituals, shout spirituals, ring shouts, shout songs, minstrel songs, slave melodies, running spirituals, and religious songs. See Bangert, 174; J. Jefferson Cleveland with William B. McClain, "A Historical Account of the Negro Spiritual," in *Songs of Zion*, 73; Jeremiah A. Wright Jr. "Music as Cultural Expression in Black Church Theology and Worship," *Journal of Black Sacred Music* 3, no. 1 (1989): 1.
15. Wright, 1–2; Lovell, 215–16, 223, 240; Cleveland and McClain, 73; William Farley Smith, "Cries of Freedom in Afro-American Spirituals," 60; Henry Hugh Proctor, "The Theology of the Songs of the Southern Slave," *Journal of Black Sacred Music* 2, no. 1 (1988): 52.
16. Du Bois, *Souls of Black Folk*, 177–78.
17. Wyatt Walker, 52–54.
18. Wyatt Walker, 54.
19. Wyatt Walker, 54.
20. While it is difficult to pinpoint the origin of the spirituals, Lovell believes that this spiritual is based on the scripture that states, "Let your light shine before others, so that they may see your good works and give glory to your Father in heaven" (Matt. 5:16). According to Lovell, the slaves were inspired to let their light shine even in the midst of darkness. See Lovell, 287–88.
21. Wyatt Walker, 55.
22. Wyatt Walker, 55. For more information on the adaptation of the spirituals during the civil rights movement, see Lincoln and Mamiya, 368–71; William Farley Smith, "Cries of Freedom in Afro-American Spirituals," 60–71; Jon Michael Spencer, "Freedom Songs of the Civil Rights Movement," *Journal of Black Sacred Music* 1, no. 2 (1987): 1–16.
23. Wyatt Walker, 55.
24. Wyatt Walker, 56–59. For additional information on coded or dual messages, see also Levine, 7–10; Lovell, 7, 40, 42, 45–46.
25. Wyatt Walker, 57–58.
26. Wyatt Walker, 58.
27. Comparison chart from Wyatt Walker, 53.

28. Hale, 193; Peter J. Paris, *The Spirituality of African Peoples: The Search for a Common Moral Discourse* (Minneapolis: Fortress Press, 1995), 34.
29. Paris, 34–35.
30. Barrett, "African Religions," 314.
31. Barrett, "African Religions," 313.
32. Ogbonnaya, 1.
33. Ogbonnaya, 4.
34. Levine, 32.
35. Paris, 33–34.
36. Lovell, 37–42; Barrett, "African Religions," 314.
37. African traditional religion refers to "the indigenous religion of the Africans." This religion, according to J. Omosade Awolalu, is still a vital part of African culture, particularly as it has been passed on from one generation to the next and as Africans continue to embrace this religion in their daily living. See J. Omosade Awolalu, "Sin and Its Removal in African Traditional Religion," *Journal of the American Academy of Religion* 44, no. 2 (1976): 275.
38. Aylward Shorter, *African Christian Theology: Adaptation or Incarnation?* (Maryknoll, N.Y.: Orbis Books, 1977), 35.
39. Shorter, 36. See also Mbiti, *African Religions and Philosophy,* and Ogbonnaya.
40. Margaret Washington Creel, *"A Peculiar People": Slave Religion and Community-Culture among the Gullahs,* American Social Experience Series 7 (New York: New York University Press, 1988), 52–58.
41. Jessie Gaston Mulira, "The Case of Voodoo in New Orleans," in *Africanisms in American Culture,* ed. Joseph E. Holloway (Bloomington: Indiana University Press, 1990), 37.
42. Lovell, 37.
43. Fisher, 2–5; Southern, 8–14; Franklin, 25. See also Lovell, 41, who includes hand clapping as a "form of instrument" commonly used in Africa and closely associated with the spirituals.
44. Lovell, 39–40; Southern, 12–13; Fisher, 2–3; Franklin, 25.
45. Lovell, 37–43. Many more elements characterize African music; however, only a few, particularly those that are also present in the spirituals, are listed here.
46. Lovell, 41.
47. Paris, 34.
48. Paris, 34.
49. McClain, 92; Christa K. Dixon, *Negro Spirituals: From Bible to Folk Song* (Philadelphia: Fortress Press, 1976), 110–11.
50. Levine, 7–10.

51. Wyatt Walker, 58.
52. James Weldon Johnson, ed., *The Book of American Negro Spirituals* (New York: Viking Press, 1925), 23–24.
53. James Weldon Johnson, ed., 24.
54. James Weldon Johnson, ed., 25.
55. Levine, 19.
56. Sterling A. Brown, "The Spirituals," in *The Book of Negro Folklore*, ed. Langston Hughes and Arna Bontemps (New York: Dodd, Mead, 1958), 279.
57. Wyatt Walker, 62–63; Brown, 279–80; Southern, 249–51; Shaw, 1–4.
58. Raboteau, 212–26; Wyatt Walker, 30–32.
59. Quoted in Levine, 42.
60. Raboteau, 216–18; Levine, 42.
61. See Raboteau, 216.
62. Southern, 149; Levine, 6.
63. Southern, 153.
64. Quoted in Levine, 6.
65. Howard W. Odum and Guy B. Johnson, *The Negro and His Songs: A Study of Typical Negro Songs in the South* (Chapel Hill: University of North Carolina Press, 1925), 247.
66. "John Henry," in Work, ed., 233.
67. Odum and Johnson, 248, 252.
68. "Captain, O Captain," in Work, ed., 237. See also Odum and Johnson for additional verses, 252–53.
69. Odum and Johnson, 246–48. For more information on work songs, see also Work, ed., 38–39; Epstein, *Sinful Tunes and Spirituals,* 161–83; Southern, 177–82.
70. Odum and Johnson point out that this particular song illustrates how the foreman of a gang often raises a question regarding the work, and this is followed by the response of the leader which "sets the standard" for the gang to "pull together" to complete the specific task. See Odum and Johnson, 262–63.
71. Southern, 151–52; Thomas L. Webber, *Deep Like the Rivers: Education in the Slave Quarter Community, 1831–1865* (New York: W. W. Norton, 1978), 37.
72. Levine, 7–8.
73. Cleveland and McClain, 73.
74. For examples of how the spirituals have influenced other forms of art, see Aminah Brenda Lynn Robinson, *The Teachings: Drawn from African-American Spirituals* (San Diego: Harcourt Brace Jovanovich, 1992), and The Alvin Ailey American Dance Theater, *Ailey Dances* (ABC Video Enterprises, 1982), videocassette.

75. Lincoln and Mamiya, 369–71; William Farley Smith, "Cries of Freedom in Afro-American Spirituals," 60–71; Spencer, "Freedom Songs of the Civil Rights Movement," 1–16.

76. Howard Thurman, *Deep River and the Negro Spiritual Speaks of Life and Death* (1975; reprint, Richmond, Ind.: Friends United Press, 1990), 12–15.

77. Thurman, 15–24.

78. James Weldon Johnson, ed., 40.

79. See Thurman, 19–24. The lyrics in this spiritual "Ride On, King Jesus" are slightly different from those quoted for the same song later in this book (see page 104 below). As indicated earlier, common among the spirituals is their ability to change depending on the time, place, and circumstances under which the songs are created or sung. Different versions of other spirituals are also quoted in this text to represent various renditions of the songs and to further emphasize their improvisational and spontaneous nature.

80. Thurman, 15–19.

81. See Thurman, 25. In Thurman's view, the slaves were not concerned about the meaning or the significance of these comparisons. They were simply expressing the similarities that emerged as they observed the world of nature.

82. McClain, 120.

83. Thurman, 29.

84. Thurman, 25–30.

85. Joseph V. Crockett, "An African-American Method of Religious Education," *Quarterly Review* 12 (1992): 52–53.

Four

This Little Light of Mine

Theology and Christian Education
in the African American Church

The purpose of this chapter is twofold: to explore the relationship between theology and Christian education in the African American church and to draw implications from theological and educational insights for the development of a triple-heritage model of Christian education. To this end, I examine the relationship between Christian education and two contemporary theologies — black theology and womanist theology; I then discuss implications for Christian education in the African American church.

Black Theology, Womanist Theology, and Christian Education

Religious education scholars essentially agree that an intimate relationship exists between theology and Christian education.[1] To put it more pointedly, many believe that Christian education is theological education. This dynamic education can deepen one's relationship with God, facilitate understanding in light of this relationship, and empower people to live out their faith in every arena of their lives. Such education further engages persons in an ongoing process of action and reflection that challenges them to continuously raise new questions. To theologize is thus to participate in the educational process because theology is the quest to find meaning in light of one's reflection upon God and active involvement as agents of God's love and transformative power in the world. As the church, then, explores new theologies, simultaneously it envisions new paradigms of education.

Olivia Pearl Stokes affirms the important relationship between theology and Christian education particularly as it pertains to the African American church and community. Stokes maintains that black theology is essential for African Americans because it challenges them to reflect on their Christian faith while engaging in critical reflection and action toward social change. Christian educators must, therefore, interpret and translate the key components of black theology into a wide range of educational strategies, resources, and practical applications.[2] Suggesting that black theology be the primary focus for African Americans, Paul Nichols deepens Stokes's analysis, arguing that both theology and Christian education must be "relevant to the experience of the learner."[3]

While I concur with Stokes's and Nichols's conclusions regarding the relevance of black theology, I argue that African American Christian educators must embrace not only black theology, but womanist theology as well. Both are discussed in more detail below.

Unfortunately, the unique relationship between theology and Christian education is not typically considered in the African American church, especially in relationship to the two contemporary theologies — black liberation theology and womanist theology. In their concern to address the experience of African Americans, both have the potential to inform and be enhanced by Christian education in the African American church.

Black Theology

The civil rights and black power movements of the 1960s provided the fertile ground for contemporary black theology to emerge. Although the civil rights movement was instrumental in affirming the liberating power of the gospel for African Americans, it was not successful in freeing Christianity from the dominant white European American values and images of God that permeated both black and white churches.[4] Because many African American churches embraced the beliefs and practices of white denominations, their theological distinctiveness was lost amidst white theologies. These theologies were particularly problematic for African Americans because they were overly rational, abstract, and insensitive to the concrete issues and concerns of African American people. Disillusioned by the African American church, proponents of the black power movement, among others, criticized the church, claiming that it was complacent, powerless, and irrelevant for African American people. They further challenged the African American church to reflect seriously on what it means to be a black Christian in America.[5]

Black theology has energetically responded to these challenges and criticisms, launching a radical critique of white racism and the inadequacy of white theologies to address the needs of African American people. Given that the experience of African Americans is distinctively different from that of European Americans, black theology reflects on the Christian faith through the lens of poor, oppressed, and exploited African American people and illustrates the centrality of the gospel of Jesus Christ to their liberation from white oppression. Black theologians agree that the gospel message empowers African Americans to fight for dignity and equality as well as social, economic, and political justice.[6]

Black theology has also called our attention to the need for accountability between the African American church and the African American community. It challenges the church to become actively involved in the life of the community and to engage in concrete action towards liberation. For Cone, one of the leading proponents of black theology, this approach means proclaiming a message of hope and freedom that is relevant and consistent with the real issues and concerns of African American people.[7]

Perhaps most importantly, black theology has encouraged positive African American identity and self-esteem. This has been done not only by embracing African American history and celebrating African American culture, literature, experience, and modes of worship, but also by affirming that God is concerned about the oppressed and actively involved in the struggle for liberation. Cone asserts that God's identification with the oppressed blacks of America, through the incarnate Christ, affirms that liberation is a continuation of God's work and makes God's mission and ministry relevant for African Americans today.[8] By raising African American cultural consciousness and restoring confidence in the liberating work of Jesus Christ, black theology has attempted to instill a greater sense of appreciation for the African American heritage.

Significant for our purposes is that black theology has reinterpreted or reenvisioned theology through the lens of African American experience in an effort to affirm that experience as well as the relevance of the Christian gospel for African Americans today. This reinterpretation of theology is clearly articulated in the following statement adopted in 1969 by the National Committee of Black Churchmen:

> Black theology is a theology of black liberation. It seeks to plumb the black condition in the light of God's revelation in Jesus Christ, so that the black community can see that the gospel is commensurate with the achievement of black humanity. Black theology is a theology of "blackness." It is the affirmation of black humanity that emancipates black people from white racism, thus providing authentic freedom for both white and black people.... The message of liberation is the revelation of God as revealed in the incarnation of Jesus Christ. Freedom IS the gospel. Jesus is the Liberator![9]

Cone also affirms this reinterpretation of theology in his description of black theology when he asserts that

> Black Theology is that theology which arises out of the need to articulate the significance of Black presence in a hostile white world. It is Black people reflecting religiously on the Black experience, attempting to redefine the relevance of the Christian Gospel for their lives.[10]

Some theologians and religious scholars have argued that black theology is not Christian theology because of its central focus on the African American experience. However, Cone insists that its central focus on the African American "predicament" as the starting place of theological reflection, in light of God's revelation through Christ, *is* what makes black theology Christian theology.[11] Illuminating Cone's argument, Willard Williams asserts that the "concept of black theology is not an opposing view in the understanding of the Christian faith," but rather it "appropriates the gospel to the black experience or life situation."[12] Thus, black theology is Christian theology that affirms the centrality of the experience of African American people and empowers them to move towards liberation.

While black theology embraces a wide range of theological concerns and perspectives, some of the central claims, as articulated by Cone, are briefly mentioned here. He asserts that God is on the side of the oppressed. This understanding of God is significant because it reflects God's identification with the oppressed and active involvement in the struggle towards liberation.[13] He emphasizes this point by focusing on the historical context of Jesus, which reveals that Jesus, like many contemporary blacks, was poor, oppressed, despised, and persecuted. The resurrection of Christ is also significant because it illustrates God's liberating power over the forces of oppression. Furthermore, Jesus is not just a person who lived in the past, but he is the Christ who participates with the oppressed in bringing about liberation today. Cone's emphasis upon the blackness of Christ, although symbolic, draws attention to the plight of African Americans and the "*concreteness* of Jesus' continued presence" and liberating work in the world today.[14]

Black theology also affirms African American personhood in the quest for freedom. African Americans should celebrate their blackness and embrace freedom as their God-given inheritance. Cone maintains that the church can facilitate the journey by proclaiming divine liberation, by actively participating in the fight for liberation, and by embodying the gospel of freedom.[15]

Finally, black theology draws upon a variety of sources, including: *black experience,* which reflects not only upon the experience of oppression but also upon African American self-determination and affirmation; *black history,* which acknowledges not only a heritage of bondage, but the movement of God towards liberation; *black culture,* which includes various forms of liberative cultural and artistic expressions; *revelation,* which combines God's revelation with the struggle for liberation; *Scripture,* which affirms black theology as biblical theology and emphasizes the biblical message of human liberation; and *tradition,* which embraces the liberative aspects of Christianity in the struggle towards African American liberation.[16] Black theology thus arises out of the particular experience of African American people and seeks to make meaning of the gospel of Jesus Christ in light of that experience.

Black Theology and Christian Education

Black theology has far-reaching implications for education in African American churches. For one thing, black theology can aid the church in shaping meaningful and relevant educational programs for African Americans. To address the ever-changing needs of African Americans, Christian education and black theology must engage in a mutually transformative dialogue to bring about liberative change in the African American church and community.

Black theology contributes to this dialogue by emphasizing the importance of liberation both individually and collectively. Theological reflection grounded in the African American experience can provide opportunities for individuals and churches to critique oppressive social, cultural, and political systems while exploring useful strategies for transforming such systems. While addressing these and other multiple concerns, the educational ministry of the church can also be instrumental in effectuating liberation and social change by developing holistic programs that affirm African American heritage, teaching skills for achieving freedom and bolstering self-esteem, examining curriculum materials for aspects of racial discrimination and disparaging images, and developing African-centered materials that are liberating and life affirming.

Additionally, black theology not only encourages the church to bring about change through active participation in the community, but it also challenges the church to engage in the process of liberation for those who are oppressed. Developing a dynamic curriculum that affirms freedom, personhood, and hope can assist the church in this process. This praxis-oriented curriculum can empower African Americans to strive for liberation with immediate practical application in the area of human rights.

Finally, black theology challenges the church to develop educational programs that speak to the particular issues and concerns of contemporary African Americans. While numerous factors may be considered for developing a well-rounded program that embodies the unique relationship between black theology and Christian education, Shockley's guidelines are particularly helpful. He contends that such a program must include *a theoretical and operational educational model* that emphasizes liberation for the oppressed. The central aim of this model is to empower the powerless to participate in the struggle towards liberation. An African American–centered Christian education program must also include *a cognitive model of learning* that lifts up the Christian faith as an authentic expression of faith for those who are oppressed. This model of learning draws upon various sources, including the Bible, history, and the Christian tradition. Furthermore, Christian education from an African American perspective must provide *a holistic model of learning,* which emphasizes the "organic or 'whole' nature of existence rather than the compartmentalization of life."[17] A holistic model of learning is an inclusive model that celebrates diversity. A Christian education program for African Americans must therefore embrace *a model of socialization* that affirms the uniqueness of other cultures. This model of socialization encourages open dialogue, free from discrimination and stereotypes among persons from various backgrounds. Last, African American Christian education must incorporate *a model of leadership* that nurtures the gifts and talents of pastors, teachers, and various church leaders.[18] Shockley's discussion is helpful in that it provides a framework for educators to engage in critical theoretical reflection on a Christian education program that is informed by black theology and which focuses on the unique experience of African Americans.

Christian education from an African American perspective requires close attention to the unique relationship between black theology and Christian education. The two need to work hand in hand to assist African Americans in developing a meaningful relationship with God, to equip African Americans to address the holistic needs within their communities, to instill a sense of self-worth and pride in their rich cultural heritage, and to empower African Americans to bring about liberation and social change.

Womanist Theology

While embracing the experience of African American people, black theology often lacks sensitivity to the particular experiences of African American women. Womanist theology specifically addresses this concern. One of the hallmarks of womanism is that it affirms black women's experience, culture, and contributions while critiquing their threefold oppression of racism, sexism, and classism. Womanism encourages a constructive, theological, and ethical reflection that moves black women towards liberation.

During the 1980s, many African American female clergy and religious scholars embraced the term *womanist* as a way of naming themselves, celebrating their culture and heritage, affirming their experience, and acknowledging their historical contributions to society and religious discourse. This move was significant, according to Karen Baker-Fletcher, because women have traditionally been left out of theological reflections on humanity, and black women "have been excluded most of all." Using the contextual experiences of black women, womanist theologians are constructing "concepts of human nature that are inclusive of black womanhood."[19]

The impact of Alice Walker's definition of "womanist" on African American female theologians is striking, particularly how it has served as a springboard for African American women not only to define themselves, but also to be heard on their own issues, to initiate change, and to love themselves and others to the fullest extent. According to Walker, "womanist" comes from "womanish," a term used in the African American community to denote a young woman who is exhibiting "outrageous, audacious, courageous or *willful* behavior."[20] Such a young woman also portrays a sense of power, determination, boldness, and liberation. This aspect of Walker's definition reveals a sense of confidence and assertiveness that African American women have always possessed but have not always been allowed to exercise, because of the threefold oppression of racism, classism, and gender discrimination that continues to plague African American women even today. Thus, the term "womanist" has come to symbolize the unique experience of African American women.

Through their writings, womanist theologians and ethicists have raised numerous issues that demand attention from the African American church and community, from African American men, from the academy, and from white feminist theologians. Some of these issues include the discomfort of African American women with white feminists and their often exclusivist liberation agenda; the exclusion of the African American female experience in the church, the community, and the academy; the lack of attention to sexual diversity in

Christian womanist dialogue; and the role of the Christian church and community in the oppression of African American women.[21]

In addressing these issues, womanist theology draws upon numerous sources, including African American women's experience, culture, and literature (e.g., autobiographies, folktales, poetry, essays, and other forms of expression). These reflect African American women's heritage, traditional practices, and contributions. Regarding the womanist methodology, Cheryl Sanders offers a helpful model that includes a reflection on black women's quest for survival throughout history, a critique of the threefold oppression of black women (racism, sexism, and classism), and the construction of a theology and ethic that fully embrace the varied experiences of black women.[22] This methodology, which emphasizes a liberative praxis, also acknowledges the significant role that history and culture play in the development of womanist theology.

Womanist theology includes reflection on God, Jesus, the church, and the Bible through the lens of African American women's experiences. Like black theology, womanist theology affirms that God is on the side of the oppressed.[23] However, womanist theology goes a step further by suggesting that black women are the "oppressed of the oppressed." As Jacquelyn Grant maintains, black women are "the least" or the "little people," with whom God in Christ identifies.[24] In womanist theology, God is viewed not only as Liberator, but also as Creator, Sustainer, and Comforter. Yet Delores Williams moves beyond this understanding of God. In her analysis of the biblical story of Hagar, Williams concludes that God has not always delivered African American women from their oppression. Instead, God has often provided a means of survival and quality of life for African American women in the midst of their oppressive situations.[25] Thus, African American women experience God not only as Liberator, but also as the one concerned with survival and quality of life.

Regarding Jesus, womanist theology deemphasizes sexist connotations surrounding the maleness of Christ and emphasizes the universality of his humanness. Womanist theology also emphasizes an "egalitarian" Christology, which empowers African American women in the quest for justice, liberation, and equality. Drawing upon the theologies of womanist foremothers such as Jarena Lee and

Sojourner Truth, Grant illustrates how this egalitarian Christology has empowered African American women to challenge oppressive symbols and images in the church and community. For instance, Jarena Lee fought for the right to preach and Sojourner Truth supported women's participation in the struggle for liberation. Thus, Grant boldly asserts that in the experience of black women, Christ "is a Black woman."[26] This egalitarian emphasis, according to Grant, challenges African American women to continue to reflect deeply on the images and symbols that inform theological and christological questions as well as their everyday lives.

Furthermore, womanist theology emphasizes the sustaining and liberating activity of Christ. In womanist thought, the incarnate Christ not only sustains black women in the midst of their oppressive situations, but he also participates with them in a "mutual struggle for liberation." In other words, as Christ works towards the liberation of black women, they in turn are working to free Christ from captivity to dominant ideologies, practices, and systems that have been imposed upon him and consequently used to oppress black women. Thus, black women do not see Jesus as the dominant world has portrayed him, but they see him and relate to him in liberating, affirming, and empowering ways.[27]

Although celebrated as a source of strength, support, spiritual guidance, education, and sociopolitical action, the African American church has also played a role in the subjugation of African American women. Womanist theology engages in a serious critique of the church's role in the oppression of African American women. Although African American women have historically made a significant contribution (e.g., time, money, and commitment) to the church, they are still restricted in many churches and denominations from certain leadership roles, governing bodies, and a level of respect that values their personhood and unique gifts. Womanist theology calls for changes in the African American church so that it embraces gender justice, egalitarian orientation, and empowerment of African American women.[28]

Finally, the Bible plays a significant role in womanist theology. The Bible is a primary resource for African American women because it embodies a message of hope and liberation for those who are oppressed. The Bible has also served as a vehicle through which African American women have come to know and understand God. According to Grant, two major sources inform African American women's understanding of God: God's direct revelation in their lives and God's revelation through the Bible as interpreted through their experience.[29] Although the Bible has meaning for African American women, womanist theology calls for a reinterpretation of the biblical text, images, and symbols that have been used to oppress African American women. Womanist biblical scholars such as Renita J. Weems and Clarice Martin shed new light on the interpretation of the biblical text when examined from a womanist perspective.[30]

In essence, womanist theology addresses the particular concerns of African American women. Its aim is to enlighten and empower African American women to participate in the struggle towards liberation. Furthermore, womanism affirms and celebrates African American womanhood, placing its beauty and uniqueness in sharp contrast to the negative myths and stereotypes that have historically been perpetuated about African American women.

Womanist Theology and Christian Education

Womanist theology challenges Christian educators to engage in critical dialogue with African American women. This dialogue should take place on a number of different levels and be informed by an ongoing discourse about black women's history as well as contemporary discourse about the life experiences of ordinary black women.[31]

Womanist theology also encourages the church to recognize and celebrate the unique contributions of African and African American women. One way that this can be done is by exploring the gifts and contributions of women, past and present, who serve as role models for the African American community. Much can be learned from the life and legacy of black women like Hatshepsut of Kemet (Egypt), the first female leader of Kemet who ruled during the fifteenth century B.C.E.; Amina of Hausaland (now Nigeria), a queen and warrior who contributed significantly to the advancement of Hausa commerce and industry in the fifteenth or sixteenth century;[32] Sojourner Truth (1799-1883), a former slave, abolitionist, and women's rights activist; Ida B. Wells Barnett (1862–1931), a writer, publisher, educator, and civil rights activist; and Mary McLeod Bethune (1875–1955), an educator, founder of Bethune-Cookman College (a four-year accredited college), and advisor to U.S. presidents.[33] Sharing the stories of these and other women can help instill a sense of pride in and appreciation of women's contributions.

Womanist theology further challenges the church to critique social systems and structures that contribute to the oppression of African American men and women. An analysis of black women's oppression would allow for the identification of racial, religious, social, cultural, political, and economic structures that inhibit black freedom and justice.

Finally, womanist theology challenges the church to contextualize Christian education. Contextualization takes place as educators explore, interpret, critique, and revise subject matter through the lens of African American experience. Sanders's edited volume, *Living the Intersection: Womanism and Afrocentrism in Theology,* is a helpful example of recent scholarship that illustrates the nature of this type of contextualization. Through their essays, various scholars examine a wide range of topics through the lens of womanism and Afrocentrism. From her analysis, Sanders maintains that theological education can benefit from both womanism and Afrocentrism particularly, because Afrocentric scholarship seeks to accomplish the following ends:

1. celebrate the achievements of African people and cultures;

2. analyze critically the hegemony of the Eurocentric worldview and ways of knowing that have served the interests of racial oppression, especially as they have skewed the self-understanding of African American educators and leaders; and

3. construct an alternative framework for understanding and evaluating human experience. The ultimate end of the celebrative, critical, and constructive dimensions of the Afrocentric impulse is, in the words of Afrocentrist Molefi Asante, to "move to harmony through rhythms that are the African path to transcendence."[34]

Thus, for Sanders, theological education that embraces Afrocentrism, particularly from a womanist perspective, must address misguided teachings and perspectives in the African American church and community as well as critique Christian symbols, images, and practices to determine whether they are empowering or oppressive.[35]

Although Sanders does not provide practical steps for implementation, her ideas for theological education are helpful. She challenges the church and the academy to reflect critically on a contextualized approach to Christian education, grounded in both Afrocentrism and womanism and a holistic view of African American heritage. This, I suggest, is a triple-heritage view that embodies African, African American, and Christian roots. A contextualized approach to Christian education, grounded in womanism and the triple-heritage, could shape an educational program that is culturally sensitive, critically engaged, and constructively oriented.

Insights from Black Theology and Womanist Theology for a Triple-Heritage Model of Christian Education

Three insights for a triple-heritage model of Christian education emerge from this discussion of black and womanist theologies. First, a triple-heritage model of Christian education must be contextualized, emerging out of the experience, history, and culture of African American people. This contextualization occurs on at least two levels. It reflects the particular issues and concerns of individuals within the African American community, with particular attention to African American women as suggested by womanist theology; it also reflects the broader issues and concerns of all African American people as addressed through an expansive black theology. Thus, a triple-heritage model of Christian education celebrates diversity by recognizing the multidimensional nature of the African American community. Christian education in the African American church must thus be sensitive to the uniqueness of everyone involved in the educational process and endeavor to explore a wide range of experiences emerging out of the three streams of the triple-heritage.

Second, a triple-heritage model of Christian education must be critical. As both black theology and womanist theology suggest, this model must be engaged in a serious critique of the barriers, obstacles, systems, and structures that lead to oppression. A triple-heritage model of Christian education must empower the church to struggle against these oppressive systems to bring about liberation and social change. A triple-heritage-rooted critique must not only focus on social systems and structures, but must also challenge Christian images, symbols, and practices that may be harmful to African American people. Developing a curriculum that engages people in a liberative praxis can facilitate such a critique.

Along with a serious critique of oppressive systems and structures, a triple-heritage model of Christian education must challenge churches and theological institutions to work together with community and ecumenical organizations to promote peace, justice, liberation, personal and political empowerment, general health, and well-being. As churches and theological institutions begin to incorporate courses, seminars, and special programs that focus on social concerns, they become better able to equip people to address the issues that affect their lives and thus empower them to bring about change in their society.

Third, a triple-heritage model of Christian education must be creative, drawing upon the sources that naturally emerge out of African American culture, such as music, dance, folklore, and ritual, as viable sources for education. These sources are particularly important because they yield powerful implications for Christian education. They not only provide material for content, but also suggest creative alternatives for the teaching process. Through these sources, Christian education in the African American church can be enhanced through applied imagination, storytelling, musical expression, creative movement, and ritual practices that are common in the African American tradition.

This creativity also demands that a triple-heritage model of Christian education embrace a variety of teaching methods and techniques and not be confined to one mode of teaching that can become stagnant and dull. A triple-heritage model of Christian education seeks to incorporate those teaching methods that allow for the greatest amount of education and draws from modes of teaching that emerge from African, African American, and Christian educational traditions. Some of these modes of teaching may include a communal learning process, sharing proverbs and parables, learning by example, and drawing upon experience.

Moreover, a creative triple-heritage model of Christian education moves beyond the classroom to an active exchange and involvement in society. This approach allows the educational process to tap into resources that are present in the local churches and communities. It also personalizes the educational experience by embracing the stories of real persons. By touching the lives of real persons, the church places itself in a better position to address the issues and concerns of the community. Thus, a church informed by a triple-heritage model of Christian education, shaped by the insights of black theology and womanist theology, can be a viable source for transformation and shine as a light of hope in a world so often overcome by darkness and despair. Embracing a triple-heritage model of Christian education can further inspire congregations to embody their God-given mission and ministry in Jesus Christ and thus proclaim with a spirit of joy and confidence, "this little light of mine, I'm goin' to let it shine."

Although black theology and womanist theology can play a significant role in shaping the content, method, and teaching process of a triple-heritage model of Christian education, one glaring weakness must nevertheless be considered. Both are primarily emerging in the academy and are not readily accessible, nor accepted, in many African American churches. Laypersons do not always have a working knowledge of these theologies as they relate to the African American experience. Furthermore, they often lack the vocabulary necessary to engage critical theological issues. Thus, black theology and womanist theology often remain academic exercises. By contrast, the spirituals are already accepted and integrated into the life of the African American church. While we must continue to examine and critique the theology of the spirituals to reinterpret them for contemporary African Americans, they can be a way to engage some of the critical issues and concerns facing the African American church and community. The theology of the spirituals is examined in the next chapter.

Notes

1. See Randolph C. Miller, *The Clue to Christian Education* (New York: Charles Scribner's Sons, 1950), 6, 15; Howard Grimes, "Theological Foundations for Christian Education," in *An Introduction to Christian Education,* ed. Marvin J. Taylor (Nashville: Abingdon Press, 1966), 32–33; C. Ellis Nelson, "The Curriculum of Christian Education," in *An Introduction to Christian Education,* ed. Marvin J. Taylor (Nashville: Abingdon Press, 1966), 160; Jack Seymour and Donald E. Miller, "Openings to God: Education and Theology in Dialogue," in *Theological Approaches to Christian Education,* ed. Jack Seymour and Donald E. Miller (Nashville: Abingdon Press, 1990), 23–24; Barbara Anne Keely, "Letty M. Russell: Educating for Partnership," in *Faith of Our Foremothers: Women Changing Religious Education,* ed. Barbara Anne Keely (Louisville, Ky.: Westminster John Knox Press, 1997), 173; Letty M. Russell, handout entitled "Methodology in Liberation/Feminist Theologies: A Theological Spiral of Action/Reflection," 1994; Letty M. Russell, ed., *Changing Contexts of Our Faith* (Philadelphia: Fortress Press, 1985), 103.
2. Stokes, "Black Theology," 97.
3. Paul Nichols, "Blacks and the Religious Education Movement," in *Changing Patterns of Religious Education,* ed. Marvin J. Taylor (Nashville: Abingdon Press, 1984), 190.
4. James H. Cone, *Black Theology and Black Power,* 20th Anniversary ed. (1969; reprint, New York: HarperCollins, 1989), vii. See also James H. Evans Jr., *We Have Been Believers: An African American Systematic Theology* (Minneapolis: Fortress Press, 1992), 3–4; James H. Evans Jr., "Black Theology," in *A New Handbook of Christian Theology,* ed. Donald W. Musser and Joseph L. Price (Nashville: Abingdon Press, 1992), 69–70; Wilmore, 192, 210–19.
5. Cone, *Black Theology and Black Power,* vii–ix, 32–33; Cone, *Black Theology of Liberation,* 4–5, 18–19; Evans, *We Have Been Believers,* 3–5; Wilmore, 218.
6. Cone, *Black Theology and Black Power,* 35, 37–47; Evans, *We Have Been Believers,* 2–6; J. Deotis Roberts, *Black Theology in Dialogue* (Philadelphia: Westminster Press, 1987), 116–17.
7. Cone, *Black Theology of Liberation,* 129–35.
8. Cone, *Black Theology of Liberation,* 63–64, 121; James H. Cone, *God of the Oppressed* (New York: HarperCollins, 1975), 120, 135–37.
9. "Black Theology," statement by the National Committee of Black Churchmen, June 13, 1969, in *Black Theology: A Documentary History,* vol. 1: *1966–1979,* ed. James H. Cone and Gayraud S. Wilmore (Maryknoll, N.Y.: Orbis Books, 1993), 38, adopted at the annual convocation in Oakland, California.

10. James H. Cone, "Black Consciousness and the Black Church: A Historical-Theological Interpretation," *Annals of the American Academy of Political and Social Science* 387 (January 1970): 53, quoted in Grant S. Shockley, "Liberation Theology, Black Theology, and Religious Education," in *Foundations for Christian Education in an Era of Change*, ed. Marvin J. Taylor (Nashville: Abingdon Press, 1976), 85.

11. Cone, *Black Theology and Black Power*, 118; Cone, *Black Theology of Liberation*, 5.

12. Willard A. Williams, *Educational Ministries with Blacks* (Nashville: Board of Discipleship, United Methodist Church, 1974), 7. See also Willard A. Williams, *Educational Ministry in the Black Community: Resource Booklet* (Nashville: Board of Education, United Methodist Church, 1972).

13. Cone, *Black Theology and Black Power*, 43–47; Cone, *Black Theology of Liberation*, 55–81; Cone, *God of the Oppressed*.

14. Cone, *Black Theology of Liberation*, 119–24.

15. Cone, *Black Theology of Liberation*, 130–32.

16. Cone, *Black Theology of Liberation*, 23–35.

17. Shockley, "Christian Education and the Black Church," 16.

18. Shockley, "Christian Education and the Black Church," 16–17. See also Shockley, "Liberation Theology, Black Theology, and Religious Education," 86–87.

19. Karen Baker-Fletcher, "Womanist Theology and Ethics," workshop held during the Annual Convocation for Ministers and Laypersons, Claremont School of Theology, November 1, 1993.

20. The term "womanish" emerged out of black folk culture and has been passed from mother to daughter. It usually refers to a sassy girl who thinks that she is "grown." While this is the main definition of "womanist" for Walker, she also lifts up other key elements that help to shape the definition. For a broader discussion of Walker's definition, see Alice Walker, *In Search of Our Mothers' Gardens: Womanist Prose* (San Diego: Harcourt Brace, 1983), xi–xii.

21. Cheryl Townsend Gilkes, "Womanist Ways of Seeing," in *Black Theology: A Documentary History*, vol. 2: *1980–1992*, ed. James H. Cone and Gayraud S. Wilmore, 2nd ed. (Maryknoll, N.Y.: Orbis Books, 1993), 321–24; Katie Cannon, "Hitting a Straight Lick with a Crooked Stick: The Womanist Dilemma in the Development of Black Liberation Ethics," in *Black Theology: A Documentary History*, vol. 2: *1980–1992*, ed. James H. Cone and Gayraud S. Wilmore, 2nd ed. (Maryknoll, N.Y.: Orbis Books, 1993), 300–308; Renee Hill, "Who Are We for Each Other? Sexism, Sexuality and Womanist Theology," in *Black Theology: A Documentary History*, vol. 2: *1980–1992*, ed. James H. Cone and Gayraud S. Wilmore, 2nd ed. (Maryknoll, N.Y.: Orbis Books, 1993), 345–51; Frances E. Wood, "Take

My Yoke Upon You," in *A Troubling in My Soul,* ed. Emilie M. Townes (Maryknoll, N.Y.: Orbis Books, 1993), 37–47.

22. Cheryl J. Sanders, "Afrocentric and Womanist Approaches to Theological Education," in *Living the Intersection: Womanism and Afrocentrism in Theology,* ed. Cheryl J. Sanders (Minneapolis: Fortress Press, 1995), 158.

23. Cone, *Black Theology of Liberation,* 19; Cone, *God of the Oppressed,* 136.

24. Jacquelyn Grant, *White Women's Christ and Black Women's Jesus: Feminist Christology and Womanist Response* (Atlanta: Scholars Press, 1989), 216–17.

25. Delores Williams, 5–6.

26. Grant, *White Women's Christ,* 218–20.

27. Jacquelyn Grant, "Womanist Jesus and the Mutual Struggle for Liberation," in *The Recovery of Black Presence: An Interdisciplinary Exploration,* ed. Randall C. Bailey and Jacquelyn Grant (Nashville: Abingdon Press, 1995), 138–41.

28. Wood, 41–46; Grant, *White Women's Christ,* 218–19; Marsha Foster Boyd, "Theological Implications of WomanistCare," in *WomanistCare: How to Tend the Souls of Women,* ed. Linda H. Hollies (Joliet, Ill.: Woman to Woman Ministries, 1991), 51–52.

29. Grant, *White Women's Christ,* 211.

30. Renita J. Weems, *Just a Sister Away: A Womanist Vision of Women's Relationships in the Bible* (San Diego: LuraMedia, 1988); Clarice J. Martin, "Womanist Interpretations of the New Testament: The Quest for Holistic and Inclusive Translation and Interpretation," in *Black Theology: A Documentary History,* vol. 2: *1980–1992,* ed. James H. Cone and Gayraud S. Wilmore, 2nd ed. (Maryknoll, N.Y.: Orbis Books, 1993), 225–44.

31. Kelly Brown Douglas, "Teaching Womanist Theology," in *Living the Intersection: Womanism and Afrocentrism in Theology,* ed. Cheryl J. Sanders (Minneapolis: Fortress Press, 1995), 150–51.

32. John Henrik Clarke, "African Warrior Queens," in *Black Women in Antiquity,* ed. Ivan Van Sertima (New Brunswick, N.J.: Transaction, 1984), 123–25; Nsenga Warfield-Coppock, *Images of African Sisterhood: Initiation and Rites of Passage to Womanhood* (Washington, D.C.: Baobab Associates, 1994), 30. For additional resources see also David Sweetman, *Women as Leaders in African History* (Portsmouth, N.H.: Heinemann Educational Books, 1984).

33. Darlene Clark Hine, Elsa Barkley Brown, and Rosalyn Terborg-Penn, eds., *Black Women in America: An Historical Encyclopedia,* vol. 2 (Bloomington: Indiana University Press, 1994), 1172–76, 1242–46; Darlene Clark Hine, Elsa Barkley Brown, and Rosalyn Terborg-Penn, eds., *Black Women in America: An Historical Encyclopedia,* vol. 1 (Bloomington: Indiana University Press, 1994), 113–28; Warfield-Coppock, *Images of African Sisterhood,*

32–33. For additional resources see also Rosalyn Terborg-Penn, S. Harley, and A. B. Rushing, eds., *Women in Africa and the African Diaspora* (Washington, D.C.: Howard University Press, 1989); Marcia Y. Riggs, ed., *Can I Get a Witness? Prophetic Religious Voices of African American Women: An Anthology* (Maryknoll, N.Y.: Orbis Books, 1997); and Jessie Carney Smith, *Notable Black Women* (Detroit: Gale Research, 1992).

34. Sanders, 158.
35. Sanders, 174.

Five

Balm in Gilead
The Theology of the Spirituals

The previous chapter noted the contributions that black theology and womanist theology can make to Christian education. An examination of the theology of the spirituals also reveals their unique contribution to the formation of a triple-heritage model of Christian education.[1]

In 1894 Henry H. Proctor conducted and later published one of the first theological analyses of the spirituals by a "credentialed black theologian." Proctor, who was educated at Fisk University and Yale Divinity School, noted several factors that shaped the theology of the spirituals. These include the potent remnants of African religion and culture; Christianity as taught by the slave masters but reinterpreted by the slaves; the worship services conducted by black and white preachers; religious instruction provided for some slaves, emphasizing moral character; slave worship within the invisible institution; the Bible; nature; and the daily experiences of life within the bonds of slavery.[2]

I'd like to summarize the influence of these factors by analyzing the spirituals in terms of what the slaves believed about God, Jesus, the Holy Spirit, humanity, sin and evil, eschatology, and Christian ethics.

God

While a variety of themes about God are present in the spirituals, probably the strongest themes that emerge are the slaves' affirmations that there is a God and that God is working on behalf of the oppressed. The enslaved community that created the spirituals believed that God was a deliverer from oppression, for God had delivered the children of Israel from Egypt. Inspired by God's actions on behalf of the children of Israel, the slaves firmly believed that God would deliver them from their bondage as well. The slaves believed, as Howard Thurman states, "that inasmuch as God is no respecter of persons, what He did for one race He would surely do for another."[3]

One notable spiritual that illustrates this belief is "Didn't My Lord Deliver Daniel?":

> Didn't my Lord deliver Daniel,
> deliver Daniel, deliver Daniel,
> Didn't my Lord deliver Daniel,
> An' why not a-every man.
> He delivered Daniel f'om de lion's den,
> Jonah f'om de belly of de whale,
> An' de Hebrew chillun f'om de fiery furnace,
> An' why not every man.

Other important ideas about God include a belief in God's ability to hear the cries of the slaves and to comfort them in times of trouble, God's supernatural power, God's self-disclosure in nature and in human consciousness, the righteousness and justice of God, and God's active involvement in history. In essence, the slaves' understanding of God reflected their African-rooted belief in a Supreme Being who is the creator, sustainer, and controller of the universe and is not limited by time, space, or circumstances.

Jesus

While the spirituals as a whole do not speak much about the birth of Jesus, there are numerous references to his nature, suffering, death, and resurrection. In the spirituals, the slaves recognized both Jesus' divinity and humanity. As regards his divinity, the slaves acknowledged Jesus as Lord, Conquering King, Reigning King, Suffering Savior, and Victorious Liberator. They also believed in his supernatural power and in his ability to work with them as well as act on their behalf to overcome oppressive systems. "Ride On, King Jesus" exemplifies this liberative understanding of Jesus.

> He is King of Kings, He is Lord of Lords,
> Jesus Christ the first and last, no man works like him.
> He built his throne up in the air,...
> And called his saints from everywhere,...
> He pitched his tents on Canaan's ground.
> And broke the Roman kingdom down.[4]

With regard to his humanity, the slaves embraced Jesus as a constant companion, mediator, and friend. Furthermore, the slaves fully identified with the suffering and death of Jesus. Because they also suffered, they identified with him personally. The spiritual "Calvary" illustrates their reflection on the crucifixion and suffering of Jesus.

> Ev'ry time I think about Jesus,
> Ev'ry time I think about Jesus,
> Sho'ly He died on Calvary.
> Calvary, Calvary, Calvary, Calvary,
> Sho'ly He died on Calvary.
> Make me trouble thinkin' 'bout dyin'
> Make me trouble thinkin' 'bout dyin'
> Sho'ly He died on Calvary.

The suffering and death of Jesus held great meaning for the slaves. According to Howard Thurman, "It was not merely the death of a man or a God, but there was in it a quality of identification in experience that continues to burn its way deep into the heart even of the most unemotional."[5] The slaves also believed in the triumphant physical resurrection and the return of Jesus, as the spiritual "He Arose" illustrates:

> He 'rose, He 'rose, He 'rose from the dead,
> He 'rose, He 'rose, He 'rose from the dead,
> And the Lord shall bear my spirit home.

Holy Spirit

Four primary themes regarding the Holy Spirit emerge in the spirituals. First, the slaves believed that the Holy Spirit was present and actively involved in their lives. Phrases such as "Jest befo' day, I feels

The Theology of the Spirituals

'im.... The sperit, I feels 'im. The sperit, I feels 'im!"[6] and "Oh, I feel the spirit moving,..." reflect the slaves' intimate relationship with the Spirit of God. Through this relationship, the slaves affirmed that they could not only feel the presence of the Spirit, but that they were also inspired to respond to the movement of the Spirit in their lives. For the slaves, a common response to the Spirit was prayer, as the words "Ev'ry time I feel the Spirit moving in my heart, I will pray" illustrate.

Second, the slaves believed that the Holy Spirit was central to their faith conversion. Referring to the Holy Spirit as "the heavenly breeze," the slaves sang:

> If you want to catch the heavenly breeze,
> Go down in the valley on your knees;
> Go bow your knees upon the ground,
> An' ask the Lord to turn you 'round.[7]

The conversion experience, according to Raboteau, was often accompanied by a sense of "anxiety" or "mourning" before "comin' through."[8] This experience often required anxiety-ridden sinners to diligently seek the Lord, "Go down in de Lonesome Valley, To meet my Jesus dere!"[9] and to wait patiently upon the Lord, "Jesus call you. Go in de wilderness, To wait upon de Lord."[10] The ultimate hope of conversion was to reach their heavenly home. "When I was a mourner jus' like you, I want to go to heaven when I die, fast and I prayed till I came thro', For I want to go to heaven when I die...."[11]

The third theme that emerges regarding the Holy Spirit is the slaves' belief that the Spirit initiated and empowered worship. For the enslaved community, the Spirit enabled the preaching, singing, praying, shouting, and genuine response to the presence of God. The following spiritual illustrates:

> I'm gonna sing when the Spirit says a-Sing,
> I'm gonna sing when the Spirit says a-Sing,
> I'm gonna sing when the Spirit says a-Sing,
> And obey the Spirit of the Lord.

The verses repeat, replacing the word "sing" with "shout," "preach," and "pray." As Costen notes, the outpouring of the Spirit of God upon the slaves empowered both their personal and corporate worship experience.[12] This experience was significant because it created an environment for the slaves not only to worship God, but also to express the cares and concerns of the community in worship.

Fourth, the spirituals reveal that the Holy Spirit provided the slaves with comfort, wisdom, discernment, and strength to endure the hardships of bondage. The spiritual "Balm in Gilead" embodies these themes.

> There is a balm in Gilead, to make the wounded whole,
> There is a balm in Gilead, to heal the sin-sick soul.
>
> Sometimes I feel discouraged, And think my work's in vain,
> But then the Holy Spirit Revives my soul again.
>
> Don't ever feel discouraged, For Jesus is your friend,
> And if you look for knowledge, He'll ne'er refuse to lend.
>
> If you cannot preach like Peter, If you cannot pray like Paul,
> You can tell the love of Jesus, And say "He died for all."

The Holy Spirit played an integral role in the life of the enslaved community. In the invisible institution, the presence and movement of the Holy Spirit gave birth to their creative expression in worship; the power of the Holy Spirit united the common concerns of the people; the comfort of the Holy Spirit allowed the slave community to endure the hardships of their existential reality. Although the slave owners distorted the Word of God, the Spirit of God allowed the slaves to see beyond the hypocrisy of the slave owners and to discern the true essence of God's message of love and salvation. Through the love of God, the Holy Spirit strengthened their faith and inspired a sense of hope for the future that helped them envision freedom from their oppression.

Humanity

In relationship to humanity, at least two theological themes may be identified. First, the slaves believed that they were children of God.

This belief was evident in numerous spirituals where the slaves referred to themselves as "all God's chillun'," "born of God," "God's chillun'," and "little children"[13] in relationship to God's kingdom. The slaves also frequently referred to heaven as home, which indicates their identification with God as their heavenly Parent.

> Soon-a will be done-a with the troubles of the world,
> Troubles of the world,
> The troubles of the world.
> Soon-a will be done-a with the troubles of the world.
> Goin' home to live with God.[14]

Their belief that they were children of God further reinforced the slaves' sense of their own humanity. Thurman illustrates this point in his discussion about the antebellum black preacher who was responsible for the overall spiritual development of the slave community. According to Thurman, the preacher's primary responsibility was to remind the slaves that they were created in God's image and were, therefore, children of God.[15]

Second, the slaves expressed a longing for freedom, not only in reference to trials, tribulations, sin, and evil, but also in regards to slavery. As suggested above, this longing for freedom was often expressed as a desire for death. Thurman's comments on freedom emphasize this point as he states, "Freedom from slavery and freedom from life were often synonymous in the thought of those early singers. With actual freedom no closer,... death seemed the only hope."[16] Again, "O Freedom" illustrates the slaves' desire to be free:

> O freedom! O freedom!
> O freedom over me!
> An' befo' I'd be a slave,
> I'll be buried in my grave,
> An' go home to my Lord an' be free.[17]

There has been some debate about the otherworldliness focus of the spirituals, particularly given that numerous spirituals reflect the slaves' desire to leave this world of trouble for a more blissful place (heaven) that is free from the trials and tribulations of this world. While some argue that this focus did not motivate the slaves to strive for their earthly freedom, others, such as James Cone and Dwight Hopkins, argue to the contrary. They maintain that the slaves' hope for freedom was not only a desire for something outside of their reality, but it was also a desire for freedom in terms of liberation from the temporal bonds of slavery.[18] Dwight Hopkins emphasizes this point by suggesting that because the slaves knew that they were created to be free and recognized their "God-given humanity," this realization encouraged them to affirm and strive for their freedom.[19]

Sin and Evil

Several themes arise in relationship to sin and evil. The slaves saw Satan as a real being who was associated with evil. He was depicted in many of the spirituals as a crafty, deceitful "snake in the grass,"[20] who was the source of all sin and evil in the world. The slaves also referred to Satan as a conjurer, who operated in the spiritual realm of evil, as expressed in "O, Satan is a liar, and he conjure too, And if you don't mind, he'll conjure you."[21] This notion of a conjurer can be traced to the African belief that a conjurer was a person of mystical power who was "two-faced" or "two-handed": he or she either worked for good or evil. Because the slaves believed that any type of disaster, destruction, or unusual illness was the result of "another's animosity" or "conjure," it is easy to see how the slaves readily adapted this view and applied it to Satan.[22] Thus, Satan was perceived not only as an "arch-enemy of the soul," but also as an "enemy of all righteousness," whose kingdom had to be destroyed.[23]

Cone expands this view of Satan by suggesting that he represented more than just a being who embodied evil; he also represented all aspects of the evil institution of slavery. He maintains that the slaves associated their own experience of oppression with the activity of Satan, whom they believed was the "Evil One" portrayed in the Bible. Thus, they understood Satan not only as one who perpetuates sin and evil, but also as one whose influence pervades the evil structures in the world, including those structures that supported slavery.[24] The following verses illustrate the connection the slaves made between Satan and slavery.

> Ole Satan like dat hunting dog,
> He hunt dem Christians home to God.
> Ole Satan thought he had me fas';
> Broke his chain an' I'm free at las'.

In this respect, Satan is given a religious meaning as well as a social and political interpretation.

The slaves not only associated sin and evil with Satan, but they also believed that sin brings about death, destruction, and eternal estrangement from God. Jesus was seen as the one who overcomes the sinfulness of the world through his death and resurrection. Thus, sinners are encouraged to flee sin and evil and to turn to Jesus. The following spiritual, entitled "Come, Sinner, Come," illustrates this invitation to come to Jesus.

> Won't you come, won't you come?
> Come, sinner, come;
> Great day of wrath is comin';
> Come, sinner, come.
> Look over yonder what I see;
> Come, sinner, come;
> Two tall angels comin' after me;
> Come, sinner, come.

Although sin and evil were manifested in a variety of ways, the slaves held firm to their belief that the sins of this world could be overcome through the power of Jesus.

Eschatology

The spirituals contain numerous references to heaven, hell, judgment, and the resurrection. Heaven is portrayed as a beautiful, blissful place where the righteous go to be with Jesus. It is also a place without pain and sorrow, trials and tribulations, or the pressures of this world. Hell, on the other hand, is a place of eternal punishment for Satan and his followers. In the spirituals, eternal torment is described as the punishment for the wicked, while eternal bliss is the reward for the righteous. The Judgment Day signifies the return of Jesus to judge everyone, including the living and the dead. Drawing from the description in the Bible, the slaves believed that everyone would have to stand before the "judgment bar" and give an account of their actions on earth.[25]

> You'd better min' how you talk,
> you'd better min' what you talkin' about,
> You got to give account in de Judgment,
> you'd better min'.

In terms of the resurrection, the slaves believed not only in Jesus' resurrection, but also in the resurrection of the righteous. The slaves' eschatology also reveals a strong otherworldly emphasis. However, on this point Cone argues that the references to "heaven" and the "promised land," in some spirituals, actually carried a double meaning. Thus, these references represented a coded message for a specific place of escape. He also maintains that this understanding of the coded message within the spirituals illustrates the desire and actions on the part of some slaves to liberate themselves from their earthly bondage.[26] "All God's Chillun Got Wings" illustrates the slaves' notion of heaven as well as their use of a coded message.

> I got a robe, you got a robe,
> All o' God's Chillun got a robe.
> When I get to heab'n I'm goin' to put on my robe,
> I'm goin' to shout all ovah God's Heab'n,...
> Ev'rybody talkin' 'bout heab'n ain't goin' dere;
> Heab'n, Heab'n, I'm goin' to shout all ovah God's Heab'n.

This spiritual also seems to illustrate a sense of continuity between heaven and earth, particularly given that this concept embraces the African concept of sacredness, which views all of reality as sacred. Although the slaves were still on earth, they saw themselves as "God's chillun" who were included in God's love and plan for salvation. The reward for their faithfulness on earth was the joy of "heab'n" and all of its benefits.

Christian Ethics

Living ethically is a constant theme in the spirituals. One needs to "live right," to "trust God," to "lay down sinful ways," to pray, to serve God faithfully, to be "born-again," to live in relationship with Jesus, to respect others, to bear one another's burdens, and to avoid hypocrisy. Throughout is the acknowledgment that the Christian life is a journey as well as a growing process and, most importantly, that the Bible is a guidebook for the journey.

The following spiritual illustrates the slaves' view of the Bible.

> For in dat Bible you will see,
> Jesus died fer you an' me.
> Matthew, Mark, Luke an' John
> Tell me where my Master's gone.
> Go read de fifth of Matthew
> An' read de chapter through,
> It is de guide to Christians,
> An' tell 'em what to do.
> Now take yo' Bible an' read it through,
> An' ev'y word you fin' is true.

In his discussion of the spirituals, Proctor describes the slaves' view of the Christian life as "a life of dependence, of trust, of service and communion; a life linked with God, the Infinite One."[27] Although the slaves' view of the Christian life sustained them in their hope for freedom, it is important to note that the Christian life was not merely a passive life, but a life of action and involvement in the struggle for liberation.

The theology that arises out of the spirituals is certainly rich and warrants a deeper analysis. A greater understanding of the spirituals can assist in theological and pedagogical construction.

Insights from the Spirituals for a Triple-Heritage Model of Christian Education

The spirituals can be employed as a vital component in developing a Christian education program that focuses on the triple-heritage. The spirituals can be a means through which the entire life and ministry of the church can center on the presence of God. As congregations engage in singing the spirituals, persons can be awakened to the reality of God and new life in Christ. The spirituals can also inspire a greater sense of spirituality by moving persons towards a deeper relationship with God, self, and others. The spirituals further provide opportunities for persons to share their own stories and to witness in song to God's presence and active involvement in their individual and communal lives. Sharing stories in song is a powerful way for persons to move beyond an abstract reflection of God to a concrete encounter with the Divine.

Second, the spirituals can encourage African Americans to remember their past with all of the hurt, pain, and sorrow that it embodies, but with the assurance that communal remembering can help to bring about healing and wholeness. Maria Harris refers to such remembering, which encourages both individual and communal involvement, as mythic remembering: "gazing at what originally terrifies, and turning it into a symbol of hope and new life."[28] Remembering can inspire within African Americans a sense of connection with African and African American ancestors, a deep respect for the legacy that they have left behind, and a renewed sense of hope for the future. In this sense, the spirituals can serve as a balm in Gilead, to make whole again those who have been broken and bruised and to facilitate a process of healing and renewal for all who are striving to overcome myriad systems of discrimination and oppression.

Spirituals can further assist African Americans in remembering their past by providing a more culturally and historically significant alternative to contemporary worship songs. For example, while many praise songs prepare the congregation for worship, they tend to focus primarily upon the universal presence of God. The spirituals and the theology undergirding them, however, inspire a deeper reflection upon God's particular involvement in the life of the African American community throughout history. Although praise songs can play a significant role in the African American church, the spirituals encourage African Americans to celebrate their full heritage as they remember God's active presence and involvement.

Third, the spirituals and their rich theology can inspire a deeper sense of community, true *koinonia*, where people genuinely love, nurture, and support one another. This bond of fellowship, which was evident in the enslaved community, can empower unity and self-determination in the continued struggle for liberation and social change. Communal fellowship evoked in song can also encourage persons to reach out to one another in an effort to stand in solidarity with all oppressed people in the world. In this sense, God's redemption and liberation in Jesus Christ become both spiritual as well as social activities.

Spirituals can nurture a communal environment and a vision for social change by exploring African, African American, and Christian strategies that have been effective in bringing about communal transformation. The spirituals can thus equip African Americans to participate in concrete ways in the life of their communities. The emphasis of the spirituals, however, is not solely on external relationships; rather, they provide a way of helping people recognize and bond more deeply and intimately with the African, African American, and Christian communities of past and present.

Fourth, the spirituals and their theology can help African Americans gain a deeper sense of pride in their triple-heritage as Africans, African Americans, and Christians. Consequently, one of the major tasks of an African American model of Christian education is to encourage African Americans to celebrate their full heritage by reflecting upon each element of the triple-heritage.

Finally, the spirituals and their theology can be a valuable source for moving the African American church towards a Spirit-centered triple-heritage model of Christian education. The spirituals can enable the church not only to center upon the Holy Spirit, but also to engage more fully with the movement of the Spirit. This mutual interaction with the Holy Spirit was evident in the enslaved community. For instance, in the slave community, the use of the spirituals in the invisible institution facilitated awareness of the presence of the Holy Spirit. As the entire congregation joined together in song, they were intimately united. According to Costen, the movement of the Holy Spirit through music and song invited African Americans into a deeper relationship with God and each other. Costen further notes that singing "provides a divine channel through which God speaks and believers respond."[29] She goes on to suggest, "Singing has a mysterious power that frees the human spirit so that the Spirit of God can penetrate and, in the words of James Cone, also 'intensify the power of the Spirit's presence with the people.'"[30]

The purpose of Spirit-centered education is "to deepen persons' capacities to see and to be taken by the reconciling activity of God in our world and in our lives and to empower persons' capacities to participate in that activity with an increasingly free fluidity."[31] The spirituals and the theology they embody fulfill this criterion. Fully engaging the spirituals and their theology as embodiments of the triple-heritage is one way that the African American church can participate more freely with the Spirit and bring about a fuller fellowship with God, self, nature, and the world. To this end, the next chapter explores a variety of ways that the spirituals can be used to teach the triple-heritage.

Notes

1. For an additional discussion on the theology of the spirituals, see my article Yolanda Y. Smith, "He Still Wid Us — Jesus: The Musical Theology of the Spirituals," *Christian History* 18, no. 2 (1999): 18–19.

2. Proctor, 51–52, 57–58, 63.

3. Thurman, 15.

4. See Lovell, 231. See also "Ride On, King Jesus," in *Songs of Zion*, 77, for a variation on the words.

5. Thurman, 21.

6. See Raboteau, 260.

7. See Proctor, 55.

8. Raboteau, 253, 266–67.

9. Raboteau, 254.

10. Raboteau, 254.

11. See Raboteau, 254–55.

12. Costen, 40.

13. See for example, "I've Got a Robe," "De Gospel Train," "Climbin' Up d' Mountain," "Free At Last," in *Songs of Zion*, 82, 116, 120, 80; "All God's Chillun Got Wings" and "Hallelujah!" in James Weldon Johnson, ed., 71, 172–73; "Chillun, Did You Hear When Jesus Rose?" in Dixon, 78.

14. See also "City Called Heaven," "Trampin'," "Swing Low, Sweet Chariot," and "Tryin' to Get Home," in *Songs of Zion*, 135, 111, 104, 130.

15. Thurman, 11–12.

16. Thurman, 29.
17. See Thurman, 29.
18. Cone, *Spirituals and the Blues,* 78–87; Hopkins, 29–32.
19. Hopkins, 29–32.
20. Proctor, 59; Odum and Johnson, 39.
21. "Blow Your Trumpet, Gabriel," in Thomas Wentworth Higginson, "Slave Songs and Spirituals," in *Afro-American Religious History: A Documentary Witness,* ed. Milton C. Sernett (Durham, N.C.: Duke University Press, 1985), 123. See also Raboteau, 257, and Odum and Johnson, 39.
22. Raboteau, 275–84.
23. Proctor, 59. See also Odum and Johnson, 38–42.
24. Cone, *Spirituals and the Blues,* 71–73.
25. For scripture references related to the judgment, see Matt. 19:28–29; Matt. 25:31–46; John 5:24–32; Acts 17:30–31; 2 Cor. 5:10, 21.
26. Cone, *Spirituals and the Blues,* 78–82.
27. Proctor, 56.
28. Maria Harris, *Women and Teaching: Themes for a Spirituality of Pedagogy* (New York: Paulist Press, 1988), 34.
29. Costen, 44.
30. Costen, 45.
31. Rogers, 5.

Six

Let Us Break Bread Together
Using the Spirituals to Teach the Triple-Heritage

This chapter is intended to offer some practical suggestions for teaching the three streams of the triple-heritage through the spirituals. Every aspect of the triple-heritage contributes to the content and teaching process of a triple-heritage model. Because content and process are so deeply related in the spirituals, they are not distinguished in this discussion of the model. By reflecting on the spirituals, numerous possibilities emerge for subject matter and for creative approaches to the educational process. The spirituals actually embody several educational qualities. Some of these qualities — dialogue, imagination, spontaneity, rhythm, narrative, nature, and ritual — guide our further exploration of the triple-heritage.[1]

Dialogue

As in Africa, music played an important role in the slave community, particularly since it permeated all aspects of life — work, play, leisure, religious observances, and artistic expression. On a deeper level, music was a vehicle for the slaves to express their criticism, inner feelings, unvoiced desires, and aspirations.

> No more auction block for me,
> No more, No more,
> No more auction block for me,
> Many thousand gone.

Music not only allowed the slaves to express their thoughts and feelings, but more specifically, many spirituals, embodying a dialogical or call-and-response quality, enabled the slaves to communicate among themselves.

> Leader: Get you ready, there's a
> Response: meeting here tonight,
> Leader: Come along, there's a
> Response: meeting here tonight.

Finally, the spirituals, expressed in the form of prayer, allowed the slaves to share their cares and concerns with God.

> Someone's cryin', Lord,
> Kum ba yah,
> Oh, Lord,
> Kum ba yah.[2]

By reflecting on the dialogical nature of the spirituals, we can explore the African aspect of the triple-heritage and consider how dialogue was used in African music as a form of communication and critique. Levine notes that a common practice among African peoples was to convey their sentiments regarding their neighbors and governing officials in an open forum, through music, dance, metaphor, and other modes of artistic expression without fear of reprisal.[3] Exploring the dialogue in spirituals also reveals the influence of African music on African American music and culture, especially on gospel music, jazz, blues, hip-hop, dance, literature, and art. We can discover a dialogue within the music and art but also a dialogue among African people, across cultures and generations. Finally, the dialogical quality of the spirituals reveals the strength of dialogical prayer in the Christian heritage. Spirituals such as "Kum Ba Yah, My Lord" and "Lord, I Want to Be a Christian" are actual prayers in song; studying them may spark numerous questions for discussion. For example, what is prayer? What kind of dialogue is it? How does one pray? This approach could lead also to a study of prayers in the Bible, of personal and communal prayer, and of prayer in various African, African American, and Christian communities.

Dialogue through the spirituals may suggest several approaches to the teaching process, such as choral reading, antiphonal and responsive reading, litany,[4] large and small group discussion, and role play.

For example, choral reading can be a dramatic way of presenting historical information, narratives, poetry, songs, and stories that emerge from the three streams of the triple-heritage.

Choral Reading

The following presentation of James Weldon Johnson's poem "O Black and Unknown Bards" could provide a powerful choral reading.

> O black and unknown bards of long ago,
> How came your lips to touch the sacred fire?
> How, in your darkness, did you come to know
> The power and beauty of the minstrel's lyre?
> Who first from midst his bonds lifted his eyes?
> Who first from out the still watch, lone and long,
> Feeling the ancient faith of prophets rise
> Within his dark-kept soul, burst into song?
> Heart of what slave poured out such melody
> As "Steal away to Jesus"? On its strains
> His spirit must have nightly floated free,
> Though still about his hands he felt his chains.
> Who heard great "Jordan roll"? Whose starward eye
> Saw chariot "swing low"? And who was he
> That breathed that comforting, melodic sigh,
> "Nobody knows de trouble I see"?[5]

Such a reading could be developed by assigning several persons and/or groups various lines to read from the poem. An outline for this reading may consist of the following parts:

All:	Lines one and two
Group 1:	Lines three and four
Group 2:	Line five
Group 3:	Lines six, seven, and eight
Solo 1:	Lines nine, ten, eleven, and twelve
Solo 2:	Lines thirteen, fourteen, and fifteen
All:	Line sixteen

This reading may be followed by a moment of silent reflection and small group discussions of the images that may have emerged from the reading. Participants may also be asked to create (individually or as a group) a song, dance, or prayer based on the poem.

Musical/Speech Choir

Another way of exploring the dialogical process of education could be through a musical choir and a speech choir that would present Johnson's poem through music and speech. In this presentation, the musical choir would sing the spirituals mentioned in the poem and the speech choir would recite the stanzas from the poem. Such a presentation may include the following:

Musical Choir:	Sings "Steal Away"
Speech Choir:	Recites the first stanza
Musical Choir:	Sings "Roll, Jordan Roll"
Speech Choir:	Recites the second and third stanzas
Musical Solo:	Sings "Nobody Knows the Trouble I See"
Speech Choir:	Recites the fourth and fifth stanzas
Musical Choir:	Sings "Go Down, Moses"
Speech Choir:	Recites the sixth stanza
Musical Choir:	Sings "Swing Low, Sweet Chariot"

The spirituals can inspire a dialogical approach to education that encourages active participation from everyone involved in the teaching/learning process.

The dialogical nature of the spirituals was beautifully illustrated in a chapel service at Yale Divinity School. In celebration of Black History Month, the Yale Black Seminarians engaged in a dramatic reading of Margaret Walker's poem "For My People."[6]

> For my people everywhere
> singing their slave songs repeatedly:
> their dirges and their ditties
> and their blues and jubilees,
> praying their prayers nightly to
> an unknown god, bending their
> knees humbly to an unseen power;
> For my people lending their strength
> to the years: to the gone years

and the now years and the
maybe years, washing ironing cooking
scrubbing sewing mending hoeing plowing digging
planting pruning patching
dragging along never gaining never reaping never
knowing and never understanding.[7]

A group of five students, standing back to back (forming a circle), took turns reading the stanzas. Four other students, stationed at various places throughout the chapel, sang (either as soloists or as a duet) selected spirituals at the end of each set of stanzas. Some of the spirituals performed in this dramatic presentation included "Steal Away," "Swing Low, Sweet Chariot," "Done Made My Vow to the Lord," and "We Shall Overcome." The presentation ended with a moment of silent reflection.

Imagination

The imagery in some of the spirituals is striking. The word pictures that emerge draw upon the imagination in such a way that the listener feels a sense of presence and involvement with the events portrayed in these songs. The spiritual "Somebody's Knocking at Your Door" beautifully illustrates this point.

Somebody's knocking at your door,
Somebody's knocking at your door,
O sinner, why don't you answer?
Somebody's knocking at your door.

The spirituals inspire us to embrace imagination as a viable mode of education. Maria Harris maintains that imagination is the "heart of teaching" and that it offers a wealth of possibilities for education.[8] These possibilities emerge as educators tap into the beauty, creativity, and transformative power embodied in the imagination of human beings. Harris further argues that an artistic approach to education — drawing upon poetry, dance, metaphor, literature, pantomime, music, embodiment, and drama — may facilitate deeper learning of theoretical ideas than a simple lecture or dialogue. She notes, for instance, that "a presentation of *Fiddler on the Roof*,... might teach more about the pain involved in commitment and conviction than a more discursive course."[9]

The spirituals also inspire an artistic approach to education. By drawing upon the imagination of the enslaved Africans, we can explore a variety of artistic approaches that probe deeply into the creative nature of the triple-heritage.

Dramatic Presentation

The spiritual "Calvary," which is a retelling of Jesus' crucifixion, may inspire an exploration of Jesus' death on the cross through a dramatic presentation.

> Calvary, Calvary, Calvary,
> Calvary, Calvary, Calvary,
> Surely He died on Calvary.

This presentation could be held during Passion Week, in preparation for the Easter celebration.

In such a presentation, the African aspect of the triple-heritage could be examined through the eyes of Simon of Cyrene, the African bystander, who was forced to carry the cross for Jesus (Matt. 27:32; Mark 15:21; Luke 23:26). *The Original African Heritage Study Bible* emphasizes the significance of Simon's African heritage and inspires a deeper exploration of the black presence in the Bible.[10] This exploration may shed light on African culture, customs, and practices during biblical times. This examination may also encourage additional explorations of multiple cultures and traditions not only within the biblical text, but also in contemporary twenty-first-century communities.

The African American aspect may be examined in the dramatic presentation through the slaves' identification with the suffering and death of Jesus. Because they understood what it was like to suffer, the slaves were able to identify personally with Jesus and thus saw in their own situation the significance of the crucifixion.

> Ev'ry time I think about Jesus,
> Ev'ry time I think about Jesus,

> Ev'ry time I think about Jesus,
> Surely He died on Calvary.

This examination may be expanded to a comparison of modern-day issues plaguing African Americans and their current interpretation of the suffering and death of Jesus in light of these concerns.

Finally, the Christian aspect of the triple-heritage emerges through the retelling of the events surrounding Jesus' death.

> Don't you hear the hammer ringing?...
> Don't you hear Him calling His Father?...
> Don't you hear Him say, "It is finished?"

These themes may spark a comparative analysis of the passion accounts in the four Gospels. They may also inspire deeper reflection on the themes of love, forgiveness, suffering, and sacrifice. The final two verses of "Calvary" speak to the result of the crucifixion and the human response to the death and resurrection of Jesus.

> Jesus furnished my salvation....
> Sinner, do you love my Jesus?

The spirituals illustrate the role and value of imagination in the teaching-learning experience. They readily transform a static and purely didactic learning experience into one that is dynamic and engaging. Consequently, the spirituals provide educators with a wealth of creative insights and possibilities that can make the religious educational experience more vibrant and relevant to both individuals and the wider congregation.

Spontaneity

One of the unique characteristics of the spirituals is spontaneity. As previously noted, the spirituals were often created spontaneously during worship, during the work regime, and as an expression of the slaves' innermost cares and concerns emerging from their living conditions. As the slaves endured a life of bondage, they shaped and reshaped the songs that sustained them through difficult times and inspired them to strive towards freedom.

Spontaneity was a foundational characteristic of the spirituals during the time of slavery, and it continued to be a strong quality of the spirituals even after the emancipation. Drawing upon the experience of Natalie Curtis Burlin, who deeply respected African American music, Levine illustrates the influence of spontaneity in the creation of African American music. As Burlin participated in worship with an African American congregation in rural Virginia, she recounts the following experience during a prayer service.

> Minutes passed, long minutes of strange intensity. The mutterings, the ejaculations, grew louder, more dramatic, till suddenly I felt the creative thrill dart through the people like an electric vibration, that same half-audible hum arose, — emotion was gathering atmospherically as clouds gather — and then, up from the depths of some "sinner's" remorse and imploring came a pitiful little plea, a real "moan," sobbed in musical cadence. From somewhere in that bowed gathering another voice improvised a response: the plea sounded again, louder this time and more impassioned; then other voices joined in the answer, shaping it into a musical phrase; and so, before our ears, as one might say, from this molten metal of music a new song was smithied out, composed then and there by no one in particular and by everyone in general.[11]

The spontaneous nature of the spirituals, rooted in African tradition, can still be seen in African and African American music today. During my visits to South Africa in 1993 and 1995, I observed a number of connections between African and African American worship. One of the most striking similarities was the spontaneous nature of the music. For example, in many South African churches, persons within the congregation were free to begin a song and the entire congregation would join in singing, often creating new verses and even dancing as the Spirit led them. This sense of spontaneity can also be seen in many African American churches. Although the choir director may begin a song during the devotional period, a deacon may create a new verse encouraging the congregation to continue in the spirit of worship. Another verse may be added by a preacher, and still another by a layperson in the pew. Thus, spontaneity calls the entire congregation to participate in the worship experience as the Spirit may lead. This sense of spontaneity inspired by the Holy Spirit is the basis of the spiritual "I'm Gonna Sing."

> I'm gonna sing when the Spirit says a-Sing,
> And obey the Spirit of the Lord.

The African and African American aspects of the triple-heritage may be explored through a broader comparison of the spontaneous nature of music in both contexts. This exploration may lead to a deeper analysis of the commonalities that are still present in both African and African American traditions. This study may also include historical, as well as contemporary, analysis. Additionally, the Christian aspect of the triple-heritage may offer an examination of the role of the Holy Spirit in worship. Spirituals such as "I'm Gonna Sing" and "Ev'ry Time I Feel the Spirit" can facilitate this examination.

Spontaneity not only engages the entire congregation in worship, but it may also encourage educators and learners to participate fully in the educational process by embracing each moment as an opportunity for learning.

Spontaneous Readings

A spontaneous approach to education may include listening to the reading of a traditional African prayer, "An African Canticle."

> All you *big* things, bless the Lord.
> Mount Kilimanjaro and Lake Victoria,
> The Rift Valley and the Serengeti Plain,
> Fat baobabs and shady mango trees,
> All eucalyptus and tamarind trees,
> Bless the Lord.
> Praise and extol Him for ever and ever.
> All you *tiny* things, bless the Lord.
> Busy black ants and hopping fleas,
> Wriggling tadpoles and mosquito larvae,
> Flying locusts and water drops,

> Pollen dust and tsetse flies,
> Millet seeds and dried dagaa,
> Bless the Lord.
> Praise and extol Him for ever and ever.[12]

After the reading, persons may be invited to add to the "Canticle" by creating their own psalm of praise and sharing it spontaneously either through movement, poetry, art, or music.

Pantomime

Another example of spontaneity in education may include having persons pantomime a short story, a drawing, or a song and then engaging them in a group discussion regarding the insights embodied in the mime. For example, two or three persons may be asked to silently read excerpts from Thomas Jones's narrative "How I Learned to Read and Write."[13]

> ... When I had got along to words of five syllables, I went to see a colored friend, Ned Cowan, whom I knew I could trust. I told him I was trying to learn to read, and asked him to help me a little. He said he did not dare to give me any instruction, but he heard me read a few words, and then told me I should learn if I would only persevere as nobly as I had done thus far. I told him *how* I had got along, and what difficulties I had met with. He encouraged me, and spoke very kindly of my efforts to improve my condition by getting learning.... Jacob showed me a little about writing.... These letters were also in my spelling-book, and according to Jacob's directions, I set them before me for a copy, and wrote on these exercises till I could form all the letters and call them by name. One evening I wrote out my name in large letters — THOMAS JONES. This I carried to Jacob, in a great excitement of happiness....[14]

Persons would then be asked to mime the story, acting out the script the way they remember it, adding their own insights, gestures, personalities, and expressions. After the mime, the entire group may be asked to identify with one of the characters and to express in one or two words a feeling, a symbol, or a message that emerged in relation to that character. The words could then form the basis for further exploration and discussion of historical, contemporary, and Christian themes that emerged throughout the mime.

Rhythm

Rhythm is an integral part of African American spirituals. One characteristic of the spirituals is that they are not limited to one particular rhythm, but they embody a wide range of rhythms, including slow and lamenting, powerful and energetic, rigorous and triumphant, depending upon the type of spiritual. The spirituals "Certainly, Lord" and "Ain't Dat Good News?" express high-spirited jubilant rhythms, while the spirituals "Sometimes I Feel Like a Motherless Chile" and "I've Been 'Buked" reflect rhythms that are slow and plaintive. The spirituals remind us that rhythm is a natural part of our world. Rhythms that include the sunrise and sunset, the changing of the seasons, bodily rhythms, musical rhythms, historical rhythms, and so forth can be embraced as a viable part of the educational process.

Rhythm in the spirituals can help us to explore the African aspect of the triple-heritage by examining the significance of the drums, which were instrumental in establishing a sense of rhythm as well as an elaborate form of communication in African villages. Miles Mark Fisher notes that the drums of West Africa are the "oldest original rhythmic instruments." These instruments were specially crafted and used for various purposes in the African community.[15] For example, the "ntumpane," or the "talking drums," were often made from the "skin of a female elephant's ear." These drums were unique in that they imitated the human voice and were typically used to transmit important information such as imminent danger, a call to battle, births, deaths, communal celebrations, and historical accounts.[16] An examination of African heritage may include a study of the talking drum, sacred rituals surrounding the crafting of the drum, the impact of the loss of the drum on African people, and the use of the drum in religious practices and rituals. Inviting guest speakers and drumming corps not only to demonstrate the use of the drums, but also to provide opportunities for persons to explore the drums can facilitate this discussion. This learning experience may also include exposure to other African instruments, African attire, and various aspects of African culture that incorporate the use of drums.

Although Africans transported to America were stripped of the drums, Spencer notes that the inner rhythms could not be stripped from African peoples. According to Spencer, rhythm was transported to the new world and continued to influence music, religious practices, and the inner stirrings of African peoples in the Diaspora. In his estimation, rhythm is the "African remnant of black religion in North America."[17]

The African American aspect of the triple-heritage may be explored through a study of the "ring shout," which relied heavily on the various rhythms of the spirituals. The ring shout was a mode of religious expression consisting of dancing, singing, shouting, and spirit possession. Although the ring shout originated in Africa, it also was part of the worship experience of the enslaved community in America. William Francis Allen, Charles Pickard Ware, and Lucy McKim Garrison's description of the ring shout, commonly observed in South Carolina and other southern states, reveals the significance of the spirituals to this unique religious celebration.

> The true "shout" takes place on Sundays or on "praise"-nights through the week, and either in the praise-house or in some cabin.... The benches are pushed back to the wall,... and old and young, men and women,... all stand up in the middle of the floor, and when the "sperichil" is struck up, begin first walking and by-and-by shuffling round, one after the other, in a ring. The foot is hardly taken from the floor, and the progression is mainly due to a jerking, hitching motion, which agitates the entire shouter,... Sometimes they dance silently, sometimes as they shuffle they sing the chorus of the spiritual, and sometimes the song itself is also sung by the dancers. But more frequently a band,... of the best singers,... "base" the others, singing the body of the song and clapping their hands together or on the knees.[18]

The use of the spirituals to explore the ring shout may spark a broader examination of the role of dance in both contemporary African and

African American churches. A reenactment of the ring shout, using such spirituals as "I'm Gonna Sing" and "Ev'ry Time I Feel the Spirit," may also facilitate a study of various elements of worship in the African American church, including singing, praising, preaching, dancing, shouting, and fellowship.

The Christian aspect of the triple-heritage may be explored through a study of rhythm in the Bible, particularly through the poetry of the Psalms. This examination may spark a study of the instruments of worship in the Bible, the role of dance in the Psalms, or the significance of shouting, singing, and praising God as reflected in Psalm 98:4–6.

> Make a joyful noise to the LORD, all the earth;
> break forth into joyous song and sing praises.
> Sing praises to the LORD with the lyre,
> with the lyre and the sound of melody.
> With trumpets and the sound of the horn
> make a joyful noise before the King, the LORD.[19]

Rhythm may further inspire a comparative study of the spirituals and the Psalms, exploring various historical, theological, social, and cultural themes.

Beyond worship, rhythm can also guide the practice of education. For example, educators may organize their curriculum around the rhythms of the seasonal African American holidays and celebrations (e.g., Kwanzaa, Martin Luther King Jr.'s birthday, Black History Month, and Juneteenth). This approach would allow churches to emphasize various aspects of African and African American heritage during different times of the year. Educators may also organize around the rhythms of the Christian calendar (e.g., Advent, Christmas, Epiphany, Lent, Easter, Pentecost, and other special days). Various aspects of African, African American, and Christian traditions can be explored during these seasons. Moreover, rhythm can be practiced in the designing of education by incorporating moments of quietness and activity, lamenting and celebrating, and raising questions and sharing testimonies. These moments may be incorporated in prayer meetings, Bible studies, organizational meetings, choir rehearsals, and various gatherings of the church. For example, the opening devotion of a deacon's meeting may include several moments of silence. Members may then be asked to share a word of praise and thanksgiving by reciting a litany. The devotion may close with a brief testimony from one or two deacons or with the singing of the spiritual "Glory, Glory, Hallelujah."

Five-Part Meditation

An example of rhythm in an educational setting may include engaging persons in a five-part meditation on the biblical story of Joshua's victory at Jericho (Josh. 6:1–27). After listening to a recording of the spiritual "Joshua Fit de Battle of Jericho,"[20] this meditation may include the following rhythmic phases.

I. *God's Instruction/Joshua Speaks to the People*
Reading of the text (vv. 1–7)
Singing of the spiritual "Joshua Fit de Battle of Jericho"
Silent reflection
Discussion

II. *The March*
Reading of the text (vv. 8–14)
Singing of the spiritual
Silent reflection
Discussion

III. *The Shout and the Victory*
Reading of the text (vv. 15–21)
Singing of the spiritual
Silent reflection
Discussion

IV. *Rahab's Family Is Spared*
Reading of the text (vv. 22–27)
Singing of the spiritual
Silent reflection
Discussion

Let Us Break Bread Together

> V. *Reenactment of the March*
> Discussion, reflection, and reenactment of a contemporary march for civil rights in America, against apartheid in South Africa, or other forms of protest throughout the world.
> Closing reflection and prayer

Narrative

Many spirituals tell the story of biblical characters and events. Examples of these spirituals are "Didn't It Rain," "Go Down, Moses," "Joshua Fit de Battle of Jericho," "Little David, Play on Your Harp," "Ezek'el Saw de Wheel," "Didn't My Lord Deliver Daniel?" "Wake Up, Jonah!" and "Go, Tell It on the Mountain." Narrative spirituals can be used to teach not only biblical stories but stories from various African and African American cultures and traditions. These spirituals may also spark a study of the hidden messages of bondage, hope, and freedom embodied in some of these songs.

The spiritual "Go Down, Moses" is a narrative of the Exodus story. Through this spiritual, we can explore the African aspect of the triple-heritage by examining the coded or hidden messages that emerge throughout the spiritual. For instance, because the slaves were not permitted to express openly their hopes for freedom, they masked their belief in liberation by adopting the Exodus story as their own.

> When Israel was in Egypt's land: Let my people go;
> Oppressed so hard they could not stand, Let my people go.
> Go down, Moses, 'Way down in Egypt land,
> Tell ole Pharaoh, Let my people go.

In reciting the Exodus story in song, the enslaved Africans also expressed a covert form of resistance to their bondage. As Spencer notes, "Behind the mask of the spirituals was authentic *confrontation* and *conflict*."[21] By examining the origins of using coded messages, we can gain insight into African worldviews, customs, practices, and beliefs.

"Go Down, Moses" also helps us to explore the African American aspect of the triple-heritage by examining the enslaved community's understanding of their own condition of bondage. This understanding can then be explored in light of modern-day challenges of racism, sexism, classism, poverty, and other forms of oppression that continue to confront African Americans even today. Finally, the Christian aspect of the triple-heritage can be explored through "Go Down, Moses" by reflecting on the slaves' understanding of God. The spiritual reveals the slaves' identification with the children of Israel and communicates their belief in a God who identified with their suffering and who would one day liberate them from bondage.

> Oh, let us all from bondage flee: Let my people go;
> And let us all in Christ be free, Let my people go.

The theology of the enslaved African community, as revealed through this spiritual, may also be analyzed in light of contemporary theological themes in the African American church. More specifically, persons may reflect on the following questions: Who is God to us today? What can we glean from the Bible about God today? Based on our understanding of God, what is our responsibility as agents of change in our communities and broader society?

Narrative through the spirituals reminds us today of the importance of story in the oral culture of the ancestral African homeland, the history of African Americans, and the Christian faith. Story can be a powerful mode of education because it allows persons not only to draw upon their own experience, but also to enter into the experience of others. In short, the stories embodied in the spirituals can benefit Christian education by providing insights into the faith understandings of previous generations, their use of the Scriptures in light of these understandings, and how they were inspired to live out their faith even in the midst of bondage. But sharing stories can also be an effective way to explore other cultures, to engage in social critique, and to inspire a sense of hope for the future. In addition, stories can encourage the creation of other stories. Such stories may include personal testimonies, autobiographies, biblically inspired narratives, faith stories, heritage stories, folktales, poetry, fiction, historical accounts, and conversations with others.

Storytelling

One way that narrative can be used in the practice of education is to have persons view a short clip from the movie *Amistad,* where one of the imprisoned Africans, with no prior knowledge of the Bible, recounts the biblical story of Jesus' life, death, and resurrection. After viewing this clip, persons may be asked to write or draw a story that reflects their understanding of God in relationship to those who are oppressed.[22]

Another example of the narrative process of education would be to invite people (after listening to one or two narrative spirituals) to create a collage of pictures, artifacts, or other meaningful objects that tells the story of their faith journey. The collages and stories would then be shared in small group discussions. Other possibilities for reflecting on the triple-heritage through the lens of narrative include a study of African and African American heroes and heroines and an exploration of the Christmas story as reflected in the spirituals.

Nature

Howard Thurman reminds us that the world of nature is one of the primary sources of the spirituals.[23] In the spirituals, nature is used in at least two ways: as metaphor and as object lesson. The spiritual "Deep River" is an example of nature as metaphor.

> Deep river, my home is over Jordan
> Deep river, Lord, I want to cross over into campground.
> O don't you want to go to that gospel feast,
> That promis'd land where all is peace?

The image of the river, embodied in this spiritual, may have represented the prospect of both spiritual and earthly freedom. To cross "over into camp-ground" could have meant escaping to another physical location and beginning a new life in Canada or in one of the northern states, or it could have represented new life with Christ once this earthy existence was over. As with many spirituals, the deeper message is coded or masked to conceal the slaves' profound longing for freedom.[24]

The spiritual "Keep a-Inchin' Along" illustrates nature as object lesson.

> Keep a-inching along,
> Jesus will come by and by.
> Keep a-inching along,
> like a poor inchworm,
> Jesus will come by and by.

The message embodied in this spiritual may be twofold. First, this spiritual may reflect a determination to keep pressing forward regardless of the trials and tribulations one may face. By pressing forward a little at a time, "like a poor inchworm," persons may eventually reach their ultimate goal. Second, the phrase "Jesus will come by and by" may indicate a sense of hope, courage, and power that comes through Christ. As persons are persistent in their Christian journey, Christ can provide all that they need to complete the journey successfully.

The world of nature as reflected through the spirituals may inspire an examination of the use of metaphor and object lessons in African traditions. Such examination may also facilitate a study of an African understanding of nature. For example, John Mbiti notes that Africans have a deep respect for nature and embrace it as a "friend of man and vice versa." Thus, humans strive to live in harmony with nature, acknowledging that the "destruction or pollution of nature" negatively affects all of creation, especially humanity.[25] Furthermore, an examination of nature through the spirituals may facilitate a study of African beliefs about God in light of their understanding of nature. The spiritual "He's Got the Whole World in His Hands" may begin this reflection.

> He's got the whole world in His hands,...
> He's got the wind and the rain in His hands,...
> He's got the little bitty baby in His hands,...
> He's got you and me, sister, in His hands,...
> He's got you and me, brother, in His hands,...[26]

The spiritual "He's Got the Whole World in His Hands" can not only assist us in reflecting on an African understanding of God through the lens of nature, it can also inspire an examination of contemporary

African American understandings of God. This examination may in turn spark a comparative analysis of contemporary African and African American worldviews and religious traditions. Another way that the African American heritage can be explored through nature in the spirituals is by reflecting on the use of metaphor and object lessons in African American communities and examining whether these elements are empowering or oppressive for African Americans. Finally, nature in the spirituals can assist us in examining ecological issues that are currently affecting African Americans and exploring some practical ways that African Americans can be empowered to address specific issues that are affecting their communities.

The spirituals "He's Got the Whole World in His Hands" and "God Is a God" can assist us in exploring the Christian heritage by focusing our attention on the creation stories in Genesis 1:1–31 and 2:1–25. These passages reveal God not only as the sustainer, but also as the creator of the universe, as the spiritual "God Is a God" affirms.

> He made the sun to shine by day,
>   He made the sun to show the way,
> He made the stars to show their light,
>   He made the moon to shine by night,
> The earth his footstool an' heav'n his throne,
>   The whole creation all His own,
> His love an' power will prevail,
>   His promises will never fail.

Numerous questions may emerge from a study of creation: What can we learn about God through creation? What does it mean to be created in the image of God? What does the notion of being created in the image of God mean for African Americans? And how can an understanding of God as Creator and Sustainer affect African Americans' participation in the world?

Nature in the spirituals not only inspires an examination of the creation stories, but it can also facilitate a study of the metaphors and object lessons that emerge throughout the Bible, with particular attention to Jesus' parables that employ themes from nature. These parables may include the "Parable of the Seed" (Mark 4:26–29), the "Parable of the Mustard Seed" (Matt. 13:31–32; Mark 4:30–32;

Luke 13:18–19), the "Parable of the Four Soils" (Matt. 13:3–8; Mark 4:3–8; Luke 8:5–8), the "Parable of the Thistles" (Matt. 13:24–30), and the "Parable of the Fig Tree" (Luke 13:6–9). In these parables, nature is used to draw a comparison to the Kingdom of God or to teach an important spiritual truth.

Nature In Poetry

Nature as part of the educational process can provide numerous possibilities for the practice of education. For example, in a retreat setting, persons may be asked to meditate on a poem that focuses on nature, such as Langston Hughes's poem "The Negro Speaks of Rivers."

> I've known rivers:
> I've known rivers ancient as the world and older than the flow of human blood in human veins.
>
> My soul has grown deep like the rivers.
>
> I bathed in the Euphrates when dawns were young.
> I built my hut near the Congo and it lulled me to sleep.
> I looked upon the Nile and raised the pyramids above it.
> I heard the singing of the Mississippi when Abe Lincoln went down to New Orleans, and I've seen its muddy bosom turn all golden in the sunset.
>
> I've known rivers:
> Ancient, dusky rivers.
>
> My soul has grown deep like the rivers.[27]

After reflecting on the poem, persons may be encouraged to walk through the campground in silence while African drums beat in the background. As they journey into the world of nature, persons could be asked to remember their ancestors and to reflect on parts of nature that have offered strength and hope for people of African descent. They would then be encouraged to write or draw a poem about an aspect of nature through which God's spirit touches them. Persons would be invited to sing the spiritual "Deep River" to close the session.

Nature Walk

Another example of nature in the practice of education would be to have persons collect two or three items from a nature walk (e.g., broken branches, rocks, leaves) that represent aspects of nature that have been damaged or destroyed. These items could then be placed on an altar. A study of Romans 8:22–24 could follow.

> We know that the whole creation has been groaning in labor pains until now; and not only the creation, but we ourselves, who have the first fruits of the Spirit, groan inwardly while we wait for adoption, the redemption of our bodies. For in hope we were saved. Now hope that is seen is not hope. For who hopes for what is seen?

During the study, persons could be asked to identify specific areas (e.g., contaminated rivers, waste dumps) that represent parts of creation that need to be healed and ways that they can participate in the healing of creation. People would then be asked to identify aspects of African American life (either personal or communal) that need to be healed and ways that they can participate in the healing of these African American concerns. This study may conclude with a brief litany where persons are asked to recite one by one, "The earth groans for...," followed by a response from the entire group, "Guide us, Holy Spirit, in the healing of the world." Additional verses may be added to reflect the particular concerns of individuals and the group.

Ritual

Rituals play an important role in the life of Africans, African Americans, and Christians. For instance, Africans employ rituals to celebrate various aspects of life as they occur in families or in the community at large. Mbiti, in writing of Africa, notes that these events may include "the birth of a child, the giving of names, circumcision and other initiation ceremonies, marriage, funerals, harvest festivals, praying for rain, and many others."[28] Many African Americans participate in special rituals during the celebration of Kwanzaa, Martin Luther King Jr.'s birthday, Black History Month, and rites of passage ceremonies for African American youth. Finally, Christians engage in various rituals during the observance of baptism and Communion. Rituals are a vital part of communal life because they allow communities to break bread together in fellowship and solidarity as they celebrate and commemorate special events. Breaking bread together also enables communities to affirm and support individuals as they journey through various transitions in their lives, giving purpose and meaning to these experiences. The clarion call of African American churches that are striving to reclaim their heritage and empower their congregations to make meaningful connections with their past in order to live more fully in the present and future continues to be "let us break bread together on our knees."

Music is often an important accompaniment to ritual observances, so the spirituals can assist us in examining various rituals in African, African American, and Christian traditions. The spiritual "Wade in the Water," which is often used during baptism services in many African American churches, may help us to examine African heritage by exploring baptism and cleansing rituals in African traditions. This examination may include a study of the origins of baptism and cleansing rituals in Africa, the significance of water in African traditions, and the impact of Christian rituals on African traditional religious practices.

"Wade in the Water" can also be used to explore African American heritage by examining at least three areas. First, this spiritual may spark a study of the controversy surrounding the baptism of slaves. During the time of slavery, many slave owners were reluctant to baptize slaves for fear that baptism would justify the slaves' freedom. Numerous laws were enacted to ensure the status of bondage whether or not slaves were baptized. Second, an examination of the coded message embedded in this spiritual may shed light on the meanings of the spiritual in the slave community. William Farley Smith notes that as a part of the "secret African slave cult," this spiritual probably had little significance for slave owners or for those outside of the slave community.[29] This spiritual may have represented the slaves' yearning for freedom or signaled an impending escape.

>Wade in the water,
>Wade in the water, children,

> Wade in the water,
> God's a-gonna trouble the water.

Third, this spiritual may inspire a study of the symbol of water and its use in ritual ceremonies not only in the enslaved community, but also in contemporary African American churches.

"Wade in the Water" can also facilitate our reflection on the Christian aspect of the triple-heritage through a study of baptism. This examination may generate questions such as: What is baptism? How is baptism practiced in various denominations? What does baptism symbolize? "Wade in the Water" stimulates not only an examination of baptism, but also a study of another ordinance of the church, Holy Communion, focusing our attention on the biblical teachings, the symbols, and the meaning of the ritual. "Wade in the Water" may also spark an examination of the biblical story of the sick man who stayed by the pool of Bethesda, waiting for an angel to "trouble the water" in hopes that he would be healed (John 5:2–9). This biblical passage inspired the chorus of this song, "God's a-gonna trouble the water." This examination may also include an analysis of the slaves' interpretation of the sick man's healing in light of their own condition of slavery and hope for freedom.

"Wade in the Water" stimulates further discussion on the liberation themes from the Exodus story that appear in the verses:

> See that band all dressed in white
> The leader looks like an Israelite.
> See that band all dressed in red
> It looks like the band that Moses led.

These themes may suggest further study of the slaves' understanding of God and Jesus as Deliverer and Liberator. This study may also include a comparison of contemporary theological themes related to God and Jesus in the theology of the African American church with those of the enslaved community.

Ritual embodied in the spirituals reminds us that the ritualistic process of education can be an effective way to guide the teaching/learning experience. For example, ritual may be used to gather persons together at the beginning of a learning session to prepare them for the session, and it may be used at the end of the session as a way to bring closure to the overall experience.

Opening Ritual

An opening ritual for a learning session based on spiritual gifts may consist of having persons meditate on the following statement by Maya Angelou.

> While I know myself as a creation of God, I am also obligated to realize and remember that everyone else and everything else are also God's creation.[30]

As a candle is passed throughout the group, persons may be asked to reflect on who they are as gifted persons created by God. They would also be asked to identify at least one gift that they believe God has given to them and how they might use that gift in the church as well as in the African American community. Finally, persons would be asked to write a brief prayer of dedication and to share it with another person in the group.

Closing Ritual

A closing ritual for the same learning session may include having persons stand in a circle and pass a candle to the person next to them saying, "May your gifts be a blessing to all of God's people." After each person has recited this phrase, the entire group would respond by saying, "Thank you, God, for the gift of your people." Everyone would then be asked to join in singing the spiritual "This Little Light of Mine."

> This little light of mine, I'm goin' to let it shine....
> Everywhere I go, I'm goin' to let it shine....
> Let it shine, let it shine, let it shine.

Ritual of Remembrance

Ritual can also guide the teaching/learning process through meditation, prayer, imaging, and communal celebration. For example, a learning experience designed to remember African and African American ancestors may move through the following phases while African music, a spiritual, or drumming is softly playing in the background.

I. *Remembering and Mourning*

Persons would be invited to meditate silently during the reading of three or four excerpts compiled from various interviews of formerly enslaved African and African American ancestors.[31]

II. *Symbols of Remembrance*

Persons would be asked to create a symbol, or write a song or a poem of remembrance in honor of an ancestor who has special meaning for them.

III. *Communal Sharing*

Individuals would be invited to share their symbols with the group and then place them on an altar in the center of the room.

IV. *Celebration in Song and Dance*

Everyone would be invited to join in singing a song of praise and celebration for the gift of their ancestors. During the song the group would be guided through a series of simple dance movements.

V. *Closing Prayer*

Everyone in the group would be asked to form a circle and to give a closing prayer consisting of one to three words (e.g., Blessings, We remember, Praise!, Go in peace).

This exercise may be followed by large or small group discussions regarding images or insights that may have emerged throughout the teaching/learning experience.

The educational qualities embodied in the spirituals can enlarge the educational process in the African American church. By engaging the spirituals, African Americans can gain a deeper understanding of their full heritage, while exploring this heritage through a variety of teaching/learning experiences. The spirituals remind us that various modes of artistic and ritual expression such as music, dance, art, drama, and poetry, along with communal dialogue and the world of nature, can offer a wealth of possibilities for exploring the triple-heritage. These modes suggest a wide range of possibilities for subject matter and creative approaches that move beyond lecturing and discussion as traditional approaches to education.

Notes

1. Remember that the triple-heritage is a unit with interrelated parts. However, the components are discussed separately in this section for clarity.

2. "Kum ba yah" is usually translated as "come by here."

3. Levine, 7–10.

4. Choral reading involves group and solo presentations of a particular passage. Antiphonal reading consists of one group reading or reciting a passage and a different group replying or answering antiphonally. Responsive reading consists of a leader reading a phrase and a group responding. Litany involves a leader reading several statements and a group briefly responding (throughout the litany, the same phrase is often repeated).

5. James Weldon Johnson, "O Black and Unknown Bards," in *American Negro Poetry*, ed. Arna Bontemps (New York: Hill and Wang, 1963), 1. Only the first two stanzas of the poem are presented here, but all six stanzas could be presented in an actual classroom setting.

6. I was thrilled to see the dialogical nature of the spirituals embodied in this Black History Month celebration (February 24, 2003). This powerful presentation inspired and deeply moved the congregation. Persons participating in the dramatic reading included Jerome Strong, Joan Burnett, Jane Splawn, Anthony Gray, Leah Lewis, Cecelia Jones, Keri Day, Jessica Grimes, Lyle Foster, and Brian Bellamy. Shirle Moone Childs, Gilbert Bond, Natalie Wigg, Erika Jones, and Jason Richardson also participated in the service.

7. Margaret Walker, "For My People," in *This Is My Century: New and Collected Poems* (Athens: University of Georgia Press, 1989), 6. Only the first two stanzas of the poem are presented here; all ten stanzas were presented during the chapel service.

8. Maria Harris, *Teaching and Religious Imagination: An Essay in the Theology of Teaching* (New York: HarperCollins, 1987), 3–4, 19–22.

9. Maria Harris, *Teaching and Religious Imagination*, 171. For a broader discussion of how Harris uses the arts in education, see pp. 142–57, 163–70, and 172 in her text.

10. Cain Hope Felder, ed., *The Original African Heritage Study Bible* (Nashville: James C. Winston, 1993), 1431, 1468, 1525–26.

11. Natalie Curtis Burlin, "Negro Music at Birth," *Musical Quarterly* 5 (1919): 88, quoted in Levine, 26.

12. See *An African Prayer Book,* introduction by Desmond Tutu (New York: Doubleday, 1995), 7–8.

13. Thomas Jones was a slave for forty-three years. At great risk to his own life, he secretly purchased a spelling book and taught himself to read and write. For the full text of Jones's story, see Thomas Jones, "How I Learned to Read and Write," in *Steal Away: Stories of the Runaway Slaves,* compiled by Abraham Chapman (New York: Praeger, 1971), 73–80.

14. Thomas Jones, 80.

15. Fisher, 3.

16. Fisher, 3.

17. Jon Michael Spencer, *Protest and Praise: Sacred Music of Black Religion* (Minneapolis: Fortress Press, 1990), 135–36.

18. William Francis Allen, Charles Pickard Ware, and Lucy McKim Garrison, *Slave Songs of the United States* (1867; reprint, New York: Peter Smith, 1929), xiii–xiv.

19. All scriptural citations are from the New Revised Standard Version.

20. I have used Mahalia Jackson's rendition of the song "Joshua Fit the Battle of Jericho," as presented on her audiocassette recording, *The Best of Mahalia Jackson.* However, other versions of the song by other artists may also be used. See Mahalia Jackson, "Joshua Fit the Battle of Jericho," *The Best of Mahalia Jackson* (New York: Sony Music Entertainment, Inc., 1995), audiocassette.

21. Spencer, *Protest and Praise,* 13.

22. Excerpts from other films such as *Roots* and *Beloved,* along with documentaries such as *Eyes on the Prize* and *This Far by Faith,* may also be used. African and African American literature, folktales, art, music, dance, and poetry can further enrich a narrative approach to education. Additionally, other creative ways to engage in storytelling may include the use of puppets, drama, choir performances, games, creative writing, photographs, sculpting, liturgical dance, and field trips.

23. Thurman, 24–25.

24. McClain, 103; Lovell, 330; Thurman, 66; William Farley Smith, *Songs of Deliverance: Organ Arrangements and Congregational Acts of Worship for the Church Year Based on African American Spirituals* (Nashville: Abingdon Press, 1996), 45–47.

25. John S. Mbiti, *Introduction to African Religion,* 2nd ed. (1975; reprint, Oxford: Heinemann Educational Books, 1991), 44.

26. Additional verses may include "He's got the sun and the moon in his hands" and "He's got everybody in his hands."

27. Langston Hughes, "The Negro Speaks of Rivers," in *American Negro Poetry,* ed. Arna Bontemps (New York: Hill and Wang, 1963), 63–64.

28. Mbiti, *Introduction to African Religion,* 20.

29. William Farley Smith, *Songs of Deliverance,* 24.

30. See Diane J. Johnson, ed., *Proud Sisters: The Wisdom and Wit of African-American Women* (White Plains, N.Y.: Peter Pauper Press, 1995), 27.

31. Suggested slave narratives may include Chapman; B. A. Botkin, ed., *Lay My Burden Down: A Folk History of Slavery* (1945; reprint, New York: Bantam Doubleday Dell, 1973); John W. Blassingame, *Slave Testimony: Two Centuries of Letters, Speeches, Interviews, and Autobiographies* (Baton Rouge: Louisiana State University Press, 1977); James Mellon, ed., *Bullwhip Days: The Slaves Remember, An Oral History* (New York: Avon Books, 1988); Jean Fagan Yellin, ed., *Incidents in the Life of a Slave Girl: Written by Herself* (Cambridge, Mass.: Harvard University Press, 1987); Ira Berlin, Marc Favreau, and Steven F. Miller, eds., *Remembering Slavery: African Americans Talk about Their Personal Experiences of Slavery and Emancipation* (Washington, D.C.: The New Press, 1998), published in conjunction with the Library of Congress and as a companion to Smithsonian Production's radio documentary; Clifton H. Johnson, ed., *God Struck Me Dead: Voices of Ex-Slaves* (Cleveland: Pilgrim Press, 1969).

Seven

My Soul's Been Anchored in de Lord
Insights for Building a Triple-Heritage Model of Christian Education

A triple-heritage model assumes respect for, and builds on, existing African American church communities, which implies overcoming various challenges such as inertia, resistance to change, and issues related to implementation. With this in mind, this final chapter provides suggestions for building a triple-heritage model of Christian education.

Pastoral Leadership

The first insight for building a triple-heritage model is the need for visionary pastoral leadership. Such leadership is essential because the pastor can assist the congregation in capturing the vision, which can be done by keeping the triple-heritage before the congregation, affirming its value, and demonstrating its applicability in all aspects of their lives. As members see the triple-heritage as a natural part of the faith journey, they may be inspired to celebrate who they are as Africans, African Americans, and Christians. If the pastor is enthusiastic about the triple-heritage, the congregation is likely to be enthusiastic about it as well and to gain a deep sense of appreciation for this unique heritage. For this enthusiasm and appreciation to occur, the pastor must be actively involved in all aspects of the Christian education ministry, including organizing, teaching, training, promoting the ministry, and securing resources.

First Institutional Baptist Church (FIBC) of Phoenix, Arizona, provides an example of how pastoral leadership can help a congregation capture a vision, create passion, and motivate commitment to a triple-heritage model of Christian education. In 1982, when FIBC decided to implement a full-time evangelism and discipleship ministry grounded in the triple-heritage, the pastor began by preaching sermons on evangelism and discipleship from an African American perspective. For almost a year the Sunday morning messages described in detail the purpose and benefits of evangelism and discipleship with particular attention to the African American community. Each message was delivered with passion. Members were encouraged to pray for the ministry, to share their faith, and to become a part of the vision by participating in Bible study and other evangelistic activities provided by the church. When the pastor finally submitted a proposal for a comprehensive evangelism and discipleship ministry, the congregation embraced the vision and later implemented the ministry. This pastoral vision and leadership ultimately gave rise to the establishment of the African American Christian Training School (AACTS), a biweekly Saturday school for children and youth designed to teach the African, African American, and Christian heritage. As reflected in the ministry of FIBC, pastoral leadership can play an important role in developing a viable Christian education ministry that embraces the triple-heritage.

Teacher Training

The second insight for developing a triple-heritage model of Christian education is the importance of teacher training. Teacher training should take place on at least two levels. Teachers must maintain the highest standard in their teaching by participating in teacher training workshops and seminars that allow them to sharpen their teaching skills while staying abreast of current methods, resources, and techniques. Such training should be ongoing, drawing upon resources from within the congregation as well as outside the church.

Just as importantly, teacher training should involve learning about the triple-heritage, because many teachers involved in the Christian education ministry may not be equally knowledgeable about all three aspects of the triple-heritage. Moreover, this training should also be ongoing, drawing upon experts in each area as well as community resources and appropriate cultural experiences.

Teacher training should also include prayerful selection of teachers who have a vision for the triple-heritage and who feel called to participate in a triple-heritage model of Christian education. An effective way of preparing teachers to teach the triple-heritage is the discipleship model of training. This method would involve taking a small group of teachers through an extensive training program that is designed to impart the vision for the triple-heritage, to provide information and resources regarding each element of the triple-heritage, and to explore teaching methods and techniques that would allow teachers to share the triple-heritage effectively. This group of teachers would serve as a core group of leaders who could assist with training other teachers in the ministry, securing and developing curriculum resources, designing the structure of the overall educational program, and implementing other administrative duties. These teachers can also be instrumental in helping other members within the congregation to capture the vision and join in the educational ministry of the church.

Again, First Institutional Baptist Church serves as an example of how the discipleship model of teacher training can be incorporated. While preparing the congregation to implement a comprehensive evangelism and discipleship ministry, the pastor also began to prayerfully select individuals who were receptive to the vision. These persons were invited to participate in special meetings, training workshops, and Bible studies. After about a year of extensive training, these individuals, along with others who shared the vision, became members of the Evangelism and Discipleship Commission, workshop leaders, Bible study teachers, Disciple Makers (counselors), as well as board members, administrators, and teachers of the African American Christian Training School. Today this comprehensive ministry undergirds the overall ministry of the church and is supported by full-time, part-time, and volunteer staff.

Nurture

The third insight for developing a triple-heritage model of Christian education is nurture, that is, the cultivation, development, encouragement, and support of the Christian education ministry. The church must be intentional about nurturing teachers and leaders in the program. Along with ongoing teacher training, teachers and leaders should be encouraged to participate in weekly meetings during which they receive additional information regarding the triple-heritage, raise questions or concerns, support one another in prayer, and receive assistance with lesson preparation. These meetings may also serve as a forum for teacher recognition and appreciation.

Nurture is not only necessary for teachers and leaders, but it is also essential for the Christian education program. Therefore the church must be committed to praying consistently for the educational ministry so that it is anchored in the mission and ministry of Jesus Christ and undergirded by God's grace and direction. Prayer keeps the program before the congregation, which in turn may inspire more people to become actively involved. The pastor and church leaders can nurture a triple-heritage model of Christian education program by capitalizing on every opportunity to highlight the triple-heritage through sermons, announcements, church meetings, and special services.

The congregation must further nurture the program by providing adequate financial support and resources. Nurturing the program should also include ongoing critical evaluation. A praxis model of action, reflection, and reformed action ensures the highest quality of a triple-heritage model of Christian education.

Creative Methodology

The fourth insight for building a triple-heritage model of Christian education is creative methodology. Creative methodology means that teachers are willing to draw upon a variety of teaching methods, techniques, and resources, which include drama, folklore, drumming, art, crafts, storytelling, dance, literature, music, and poetry that emerge from the African, African American, and Christian traditions.

Consequently, a triple-heritage model of Christian education will be enriched through creative methodology that allows the church to embrace a variety of learning experiences and resources that can be drawn from each stream of the triple-heritage and used to explore the fullness of the three traditions.

Creative Programming

The fifth insight for building a triple-heritage model of Christian education is creative programming. Creative programming challenges the church to move beyond traditional modes of education (e.g., classroom learning through the Sunday school). For example, a number of churches have developed a Saturday school as a creative alternative to the Sunday school. These churches often prefer Saturdays because it provides more time for actual class study and more flexibility in course options, scheduling, and programming. Other churches have implemented similar programs in conjunction with the traditional Sunday school. For instance, in addition to the previously mentioned African American Christian Training School, which meets on Saturday mornings and provides courses based on the triple-heritage, First Institutional Baptist Church has created the Christian Studies Institute (CSI), an elective program offering courses on a variety of topics throughout the week as well as on Sunday mornings. The institute even offers certificates upon completion of the course of studies.

While some churches may not have established institutes, they offer numerous courses that address both spiritual and personal concerns. These types of programs lend themselves to a triple-heritage model of Christian education because they provide a flexible program that allows members to select courses that meet their individual needs while allowing members to also participate in the traditional Sunday school if they prefer to do so.

Creative programming also allows the church to explore a variety of options for implementing a triple-heritage model of Christian education. For example, the Christian education ministry may offer courses that focus on each component of the triple-heritage. This approach is limited, however, by the fact that the triple-heritage may be interpreted as three distinct components rather than as a whole.

On the other hand, the triple-heritage may be disseminated through all facets of the church experience. The value of this approach is that it does not limit Christian education to the classroom setting nor to dependency upon traditional printed curriculum resources. Instead, it promotes the view that Christian education takes place whenever the church comes together, whether for worship, fellowship, communion, meetings, outreach, choir rehearsals, special programs, family gatherings, or Bible study. This approach also suggests that Christian education happens through music, pictures, stories, images, and symbols that might be embodied in the life of the church.

Creative programming benefits a triple-heritage model of Christian education in that it provides a sense of freedom and flexibility that allows the church to explore various models of Christian education. Although one model of Christian education may work well for one congregation, a combination of several models may offer the best program of study for another.

Curriculum Resources

The sixth insight for building a triple-heritage model of Christian education is incorporating effective curriculum resources. While some curriculum materials designed for African American churches reflect the triple-heritage, many fall short in this endeavor. Consequently, many African American churches do not fully incorporate educational resources that celebrate and affirm their African American heritage. Educators must be intentional about selecting resources that affirm and support a triple-heritage model of Christian education.

Effective curriculum resources for a triple-heritage model of Christian education should include several elements. First, these resources must fully embody the triple-heritage and present the heritage in a balanced fashion throughout the curriculum. Second, resources must draw from the wellspring of music (including but not restricted to the spirituals), stories, proverbs, ritual, dance, art, literature, folktales, and metaphors that are found in the African American Christian tradition. Third, resources must tap the rich origins and contents of the religious lives of historical and contemporary African Americans, including sources that inform their music (for example, the Bible, belief systems, and worldview). Fourth, the resources must present positive images of African Americans. Finally, resources must be "highly interactive as well as... engage the various senses, abilities, and cultural forms that people draw upon in their relations with one another."[1]

Fun

The last insight for building a triple-heritage model of Christian education is fun. Exploring the triple-heritage can be fun and exciting. As churches draw upon the African American Christian tradition, they discover various sources that naturally emerge from this tradition that can be used to stimulate fun and excitement in the learning experience. Fun learning experiences that center on the triple-heritage may involve individual class activities, auxiliary projects, family devotions, or church and community events.

An example of a church event that can be used to stimulate fun and excitement for the triple-heritage was incorporated several years ago by First Institutional Baptist Church to celebrate Black History Month. During February, schools, churches, and corporate organizations all over the country pause to recognize and celebrate the African American heritage and contributions to the country. This celebration has typically included musicals, prayer breakfasts, luncheons, lectures, basketball and golf tournaments, picnics, special media presentations, commemorative worship services, and other activities. While these events are fun, informative, and inspirational, the following questions emerge: How much is actually learned about black history and how much reflection is really done on African American contributions to this country?

With these concerns in mind, the church set out to explore an approach to celebrating Black History Month that was experiential and involved exploration and reflection on the triple-heritage through worship, educational ministries, and everyday life experiences. This approach involved all four Sundays in the month of February, each focusing on a different aspect of African American history. For example, the first Sunday focused on African religions, the second on slave religion, the third on the civil rights movement, and the fourth on African Americans in contemporary America.

Each Sunday the sanctuary was arranged so that it set the stage and atmosphere for the time period designated for that particular day. Members were also asked to dress in the appropriate attire that reflected that era. In addition, members were asked to bring any personal items, stories, testimonies, artwork, music, or any appropriate symbols that might help the congregation experience that time period more fully. The sermon, music, and order of worship were adapted as well. Each Sunday, instead of the normal order of worship, the church participated in a worship experience that was common during that time period.

This activity generated a sense of excitement throughout the congregation, motivating members to begin researching the music, styles of dress, religious practices, and general background to gain insight into each time period. It also stimulated informal discussion among the members and a sense of anticipation about the next service.

Although this event was designed specifically for Black History Month, a Christian education ministry that centers on the triple-heritage may use such an event as a springboard for stimulating discussion on various aspects of the triple-heritage throughout the year. For example, members may be encouraged to continue to reflect on and discuss this experience by incorporating personal exercises such as journaling; interviewing senior members in the community; visiting museums, bookstores, and art galleries; and participating in community events that center on the African American experience. Sunday school classes, Bible studies, and special discussion groups may also build upon this experience through class discussions, field trips, guest speakers and resource persons, and special projects designed to explore the triple-heritage further.

While incorporating new and creative ideas, the church can discover that faith and fun go hand in hand. When learning is fun, the church experiences greater enjoyment and participation by members of the congregation.

Effective Christian education programs are found where the church is not concerned solely with religious issues but seeks to address the whole life of the community, where Christian education is seen as a primary function of the church and, accordingly, where it is well integrated into the life of the church. One danger is the possible conclusion that an effective, integrated Christian education program is simply a matter of clever organization, attractive advertising, more teacher training, or better funding. But because precisely the recovery of the triple-heritage is necessary for African American churches to address the needs of their communities, Christian education programs, to be fully integrated into the church, must also teach the triple-heritage as the core of their curricula. If a Christian education program is to be integrated into the life of the church, the program will be so because it grows out of, and is shaped by, the triple-heritage. Such a program is firmly anchored in de Lord and in the rich traditions of African American religious life.

Reclaiming the Spirituals

Over the years, the African American church has been instrumental in establishing educational institutions and promoting the education of African American people. In recent years, however, the emphasis on Christian education as an ongoing comprehensive ministry within the church has declined. While some churches are making some strides in this area, many are still lagging behind. To reverse this trend, the African American church must take an active role in developing a comprehensive Christian education ministry that addresses the holistic needs of the African American community. This goal can only be achieved if the educational ministry of the church makes a concerted effort to go beyond the walls of the church, identify the relevant concerns of the community, and design appropriate programs that speak to these concerns.

One way that the church can provide a holistic approach to Christian education is through a broad-based Christian education ministry that reflects the triple-heritage throughout the curriculum. As this book has argued, the spirituals can be a viable source for teaching the triple-heritage. The spirituals allow African Americans to reflect on their African roots, their African American experience, and their Christian faith. Furthermore, they allow African Americans to reflect on social issues while challenging them to strive for positive change. The spirituals also inspire the church to examine the relationship between theology and Christian education in order to provide an educational program that is relevant and speaks to the needs of African American people. Moreover, the spirituals inspire the church to participate in the movement of the Holy Spirit in order to facilitate Spirit-centered education, which empowers persons to deepen their

Insights for Building a Triple-Heritage Model

relationship with God and thus carry out the mission and ministry of Jesus Christ.

Additionally, because the spirituals are easily accessible to Christian educators from various cultural traditions, they can assist educators in exploring new possibilities for multicultural religious education. They can also serve as inspiration for persons of other cultures to explore their own religious and cultural heritage by inspiring them to identify specific elements within their own culture that have special meaning, just as the spirituals have significant meaning within the African American community. The spirituals may also invite others from various cultures into a dynamic dialogue that involves sharing stories, music, art, dance, and various forms of cultural and faith expressions. This dialogue may promote a greater sense of understanding and appreciation for other traditions while dispelling misleading myths and stereotypes.

Finally, the spirituals can easily be incorporated into a variety of Christian education curricula. Because an effective Christian education ministry undergirds all aspects of the church's ministry, the spirituals are a particularly good resource; they can be used not only for inspirational purposes, but to educate church members through the choir, Sunday school, prayer meetings, auxiliary/board meetings, outreach programs, worship services, special events, and virtually all other areas of the church's ministry. In each setting, the spirituals can be used to raise cultural awareness and appreciation by focusing the congregation's attention on the three streams of the triple-heritage. The results include building self-esteem by sharing the legacy of African and African American foreparents, enhancing spiritual growth by drawing insights from the faith journey of African Americans past and present, stimulating critical reflection on social concerns by analyzing and critiquing systems of oppression, and motivating active participation within the community by examining the cooperative efforts of the African American community to promote education, unity, protection, and liberation.

Christian education from an African American perspective must undergird all aspects of the church with the liberating message of Jesus Christ. It must lift up the rich heritage of African American culture and empower African Americans to take an active role in the quest for liberation. The wisdom inherent within the spirituals, arising out of the unique experience of African American people, can assist the church in teaching the triple-heritage and thus enhance the overall educational ministry of the African American church.

Hence, reclaiming the spirituals can allow the contemporary African American church to sing, as their forebears did:

> There is a balm in Gilead, to make the wounded whole,
> There is a balm in Gilead, to heal the sin-sick soul.
>
> Sometimes I feel discouraged, and think my work's in vain,
> But then the Holy Spirit revives my soul again.
>
> Don't ever feel discouraged, for Jesus is your friend,
> And if you look for knowledge, He'll ne'er refuse to lend.
>
> If you cannot preach like Peter, if you cannot pray like Paul, you can tell the love of Jesus, and say "He died for all."

Notes

1. Moore, 19–20.

Publication Acknowledgments

Grateful acknowledgment is given for permission to quote from the following sources:

"Forming Wisdom through Cultural Rootedness" by Yolanda Y. Smith, copyright © 2002, used in chapter 1. This chapter first appeared as an article in *In Search of Wisdom: Faith Formation in the Black Church,* ed. Anne S. Wimberly and Evelyn L. Parker, Abingdon Press.

AACTS Parent-Student Handbook and "AACTS 1996–97 Pre K–6th Grade Program: Introducing the 'New' Middle School Program, 7th–9th Grades," brochure, by Warren H. Stewart Sr., copyright © 1996. Used by permission of First Institutional Baptist Church.

"What Does It Mean to Be Black and Christian?" by Kelly Miller Smith. In *Black Theology: A Documentary History.* Vol. 2: *1980–1992,* ed. James H. Cone and Gayraud S. Wilmore, 2nd ed., copyright © 1993. Used by permission of Orbis Books.

Pan-Africanism for Beginners by Sid Lemelle, copyright © 1992 by Writers and Readers Publishing. Used by permission.

The Souls of Black Folk by William Edward Burghardt Du Bois, copyright © 1903, 1989 by Bantam Books, New York, pp. 177–80, 186. Used by permission of David Graham Du Bois and The W. E. B. Du Bois Foundation, Inc. and by permission of Penguin Books Ltd.

List of characteristics of the African American spirituals from *"Somebody's Calling My Name": Black Sacred Music and Social Change* by Wyatt Tee Walker, copyright © 1979, 1990 by Judson Press. Used by permission of Judson Press, 800-4-JUDSON, www.judsonpress.com.

Publication Acknowledgments

Comparison Chart reprinted from *"Somebody's Calling My Name": Black Sacred Music and Social Change* by Wyatt Tee Walker, copyright © 1990 by Judson Press. Used by permission of Judson Press, 800-4-JUDSON, www.judsonpress.com.

"The Case of Voodoo in New Orleans" by Jessie Gaston Mulira. In *Africanisms in American Culture,* ed. Joseph E. Holloway, copyright © 1990. Used by permission of Indiana University Press.

Excerpts from *American Negro Songs and Spirituals* by John W. Work, copyright © 1940, 1968 by Crown Publishers. Used by permission of Bonanza Books, a division of Random House, Inc.

Deep River and the Negro Spiritual Speaks of Life and Death by Howard Thurman, copyright © 1975, 1990 by Friends United Press. Used by permission of Friends United Press.

"An African-American Method of Religious Education" by Joseph V. Crockett. In *Quarterly Review,* Volume 12, pp. 51–63, copyright © 1992. Used by permission of *Quarterly Review.*

"Black Theology," statement by the National Committee of Black Churchmen, 13 June 1969. In *Black Theology: A Documentary History.* Vol. 1: *1966–1979,* ed. James H. Cone and Gayraud S. Wilmore, copyright © 1993. Used by permission of Orbis Books.

Black Theology of Liberation by James H. Cone, copyright © 1970, 1994 by Orbis Books. Used by permission of Orbis Books.

"Christian Education and the Black Church" by Grant S. Shockley. In *Christian Education Journey of Black Americans: Past, Present, Future,* compiled by Charles Foster, Ethel R. Johnson, and Grant S. Shockley, copyright © 1985. Used by permission of Discipleship Resources.

"He Still Wid Us — Jesus: The Musical Theology of the Spirituals" by Yolanda Y. Smith, copyright © 1999, used in chapter 5. This chapter first appeared as an article in issue no. 18 of *Christian History* magazine. Used by permission.

Excerpt from, "Ride On, King Jesus." Reprinted with the permission of Scribner, an imprint of Simon & Schuster Adult Publishing Group, from *Black Song: The Forge and the Flame* by John Lovell Jr. Copyright © 1972 by John Lovell Jr.

Publication Acknowledgments

"The Theology of the Songs of the Southern Slave" by Henry Hugh Proctor. In *Journal of Black Sacred Music,* vol. 2, no. 1, pp. 51–63, copyright © 1988, Duke University Press. All rights reserved. Used by permission of Duke University Press.

Slave Religion: The "Invisible Institution" in the Antebellum South by Albert J. Raboteau, copyright © 1978. Used by permission of Oxford University Press.

Excerpt from "Slave Songs and Spirituals." Reprinted with permission of Duke University Press, from *Afro-American Religious History: A Documentary Witness,* edited by Milton C. Sernett, copyright © 1985. Used by permission of Duke University Press.

"O Black and Unknown Bards," from *Saint Peter Relates an Incident* by James Weldon Johnson, copyright 1917, 1921, 1935 by James Weldon Johnson, copyright renewed © 1963 by Grace Nail Johnson. Used by permission of Viking Penguin, a division of Penguin Group (USA) Inc.

"For My People," from *This Is My Century: New and Collected Poems* by Margaret Walker, copyright © 1989 by The University of Georgia Press. Used by permission of The University of Georgia Press.

"The Negro Speaks of Rivers," from *The Collected Poems of Langston Hughes* by Langston Hughes, copyright © 1994 by the Estate of Langston Hughes. Used by permission of Alfred A. Knopf, a division of Random House, Inc. Permission for world rights by Harold Ober Associates.

All scriptural references are from the New Revised Standard Version.

Bibliography

African American Heritage Hymnal. Chicago: GIA Publications, 2001.
An African Prayer Book. Introduction by Desmond Tutu. New York: Doubleday, 1995.
Allen, Judy, Earldene McNeill, and Velma Schmidt, eds. *Cultural Awareness for Children.* Menlo Park, Calif.: Addison-Wesley, 1992.
Allen, William Francis, Charles Pickard Ware, and Lucy McKim Garrison. *Slave Songs of the United States.* 1867. Reprint, New York: Peter Smith, 1929.
Alvin Ailey American Dance Theater. *Ailey Dances.* ABC Video Enterprises, 1982. Videocassette.
Asante, Molefi Kete. *The Afrocentric Idea.* Philadelphia: Temple University Press, 1987.
———. *Afrocentricity.* Trenton, N.J.: Africa World Press, 1988.
———. *Kemet, Afrocentricity and Knowledge.* Trenton, N.J.: Africa World Press, 1990.
———. *Malcolm X as Cultural Hero and Other Afrocentric Essays.* Trenton, N.J.: Africa World Press, 1993.
Awolalu, J. Omosade. "Sin and Its Removal in African Traditional Religion." *Journal of the American Academy of Religion* 44, no. 2 (1976): 275–87.
Baker-Fletcher, Karen. "Womanist Theology and Ethics." Workshop held during the Annual Convocation for Ministers and Laypersons, Claremont School of Theology. November 1, 1993.
Bangert, Mark P. "Black Gospel and Spirituals: A Primer." *Currents in Theology and Mission* 16, no. 3 (1989): 173–79.
Banks, James A., and Cherry A. McGee Banks, eds. *Multicultural Education.* 2nd ed. Boston: Allyn and Bacon, 1993.
Barrett, Leonard E. "African Religions in the Americas." In *The Black Experience in Religion,* ed. C. Eric Lincoln, 311–40. Garden City, N.Y.: Doubleday, Anchor Press, 1974.

Bibliography

———. *Soul Force: African Heritage in Afro-American Religion.* Garden City, N.Y.: Anchor Books, 1974.

Bascom, William. *African Folktales in the New World.* Bloomington: Indiana University Press, 1992.

Berlin, Ira. *Many Thousand Gone: The First Two Centuries of Slavery in North America.* Cambridge, Mass.: Belknap Press of Harvard University Press, 1998.

Berlin, Ira, Marc Favreau, and Steven F. Miller, eds. *Remembering Slavery: African Americans Talk about Their Personal Experiences of Slavery and Emancipation.* Washington, D.C.: The New Press, 1998.

"Black Theology." Statement by the National Committee of Black Churchmen, June 13, 1969. In *Black Theology: A Documentary History.* Vol. 1: *1966–1979,* ed. James H. Cone and Gayraud S. Wilmore, 37–39. Maryknoll, N.Y.: Orbis Books, 1993.

Blassingame, John W. *Slave Testimony: Two Centuries of Letters, Speeches, Interviews, and Autobiographies.* Baton Rouge: Louisiana State University Press, 1977.

Bogen, Marjorie R. "The Interaction of Art and Religion in the Culture of the Yorubas." In *The Black Experience in Religion,* ed. C. Eric Lincoln, 300–310. Garden City, N.Y.: Doubleday, Anchor Press, 1974.

Bontemps, Arna. Introduction to *The Book of Negro Folklore,* ed. Langston Hughes and Arna Bontemps. New York: Dodd, Mead, 1958.

Bontemps, Arna, ed. *American Negro Poetry.* New York: Hill and Wang, 1963.

Botkin, B. A., ed. *Lay My Burden Down: A Folk History of Slavery.* 1945. Reprint, New York: Bantam Doubleday Dell, 1973.

Boyd, Herb, ed. *Autobiography of a People: Three Centuries of African American History Told by Those Who Lived It.* New York: Doubleday, 2000.

Boyd, Julia. *In the Company of My Sisters: Black Women and Self-Esteem.* New York: Penguin Books, 1993.

Boyd, Marsha Foster. "The African American Church as a Healing Community: Theological and Psychological Dimensions of Pastoral Care." *Journal of Theology* 95 (1991): 15–31.

———. "Theological Implications of WomanistCare." In *WomanistCare: How to Tend the Souls of Women,* ed. Linda H. Hollies, 41–64. Joliet, Ill.: Woman to Woman Ministries, 1991.

Bradford, Sarah. *Harriet Tubman: The Moses of Her People.* Secaucus, N.J.: Citadel Press, 1961.

Bibliography

Brown, Sterling A. "The Spirituals." In *The Book of Negro Folklore,* ed. Langston Hughes and Arna Bontemps, 279–89. New York: Dodd, Mead, 1958.

Brown, Sterling A., Arthur P. Davis, and Ulysses Lee, eds. *The Negro Caravan: Writings by American Negroes.* New York: Citadel Press, 1941.

Bryan, Ashley, comp. *All Night, All Day: A Child's First Book of African-American Spirituals.* New York: Atheneum Books for Young Readers, 1991.

———. *The Night Has Ears: African Proverbs.* New York: Atheneum Books for Young Readers, 1999.

Cannon, Katie. "Hitting a Straight Lick with a Crooked Stick: The Womanist Dilemma in the Development of Black Liberation Ethics." In *Black Theology: A Documentary History.* Vol. 2: *1980–1992,* ed. James H. Cone and Gayraud S. Wilmore, 300–308. 2nd ed. Maryknoll, N.Y.: Orbis Books, 1993.

Chapman, Abraham, comp. *Steal Away: Stories of the Runaway Slaves.* New York: Praeger, 1971.

Clarke, John Henrik. "African Warrior Queens." In *Black Women in Antiquity,* ed. Ivan Van Sertima, 123–34. New Brunswick, N.J.: Transaction, 1984.

Cleveland, J. Jefferson, with William McClain. "A Historical Account of the Negro Spiritual." In *Songs of Zion,* 73–79. Nashville: Abingdon Press, 1981.

Collins, Patricia H. *Black Feminist Thought: Knowledge, Consciousness and the Politics of Empowerment.* New York: Routledge, Chapman, and Hall, 1991.

Conde-Frazier, Elizabeth, ed. *Multicultural Models of Religious Education.* Atlanta: Third World Literature Publishing House, 2001.

Cone, James H. "Black Consciousness and the Black Church: A Historical-Theological Interpretation." *Annals of the American Academy of Political and Social Science* 387 (January 1970): 53. Quoted in Grant S. Shockley, "Liberation Theology, Black Theology, and Religious Education." In *Foundations for Christian Education in an Era of Change,* ed. Marvin J. Taylor, 80–95. Nashville: Abingdon Press, 1976.

———. *Black Theology and Black Power.* 20th Anniversary ed. 1969. Reprint, New York: HarperCollins, 1989.

———. *A Black Theology of Liberation.* 20th Anniversary ed. 1970. Reprint, Maryknoll, N.Y.: Orbis Books, 1994.

Bibliography

———. *God of the Oppressed.* New York: HarperCollins, 1975.

———. *The Spirituals and the Blues.* 1972. Reprint, Maryknoll, N.Y.: Orbis Books, 1991.

Costen, Melva Wilson. *African American Christian Worship.* Nashville: Abingdon Press, 1993.

Creel, Margaret Washington. *"A Peculiar People": Slave Religion and Community-Culture among the Gullahs.* American Social Experience Series 7. New York: New York University Press, 1988.

Crockett, Joseph V. "An African-American Method of Religious Education." *Quarterly Review* 12 (1992): 51–63.

———. *Teaching Scripture from an African American Perspective.* Nashville: Discipleship Resources, 1990.

Danquah, J. B. *The Akan Doctrine of God.* 1944; reprint, London: Class, 1968.

Diop, Cheikh Anta. *Precolonial Black Africa: A Comparative Study of the Political and Social Systems of Europe and Black Africa, from Antiquity to the Formation of Modern States.* Trans. Harold J. Salemson. Westport, Conn.: Lawrence Hill Books, 1987.

Dixon, Christa K. *Negro Spirituals: From Bible to Folk Song.* Philadelphia: Fortress Press, 1976.

Douglas, Kelly Brown. "Teaching Womanist Theology." In *Living the Intersection: Womanism and Afrocentrism in Theology,* ed. Cheryl J. Sanders, 147–55. Minneapolis: Fortress Press, 1995.

Du Bois, William Edward Burghardt. "Pan-Africa and New Racial Philosophy." In *The Seventh Son: The Thought and Writings of W. E. B. Du Bois,* ed. Julius Lester, 205–9. Vol. 2. New York: Random House, 1971.

———. *The Souls of Black Folk.* 1903. Reprint, New York: Bantam Books, 1989.

Epstein, Dena J. *Sinful Tunes and Spirituals: Black Folk Music to the Civil War.* Music in American Life. Urbana: University of Illinois Press, 1977.

———. "A White Origin for the Black Spirituals? An Invalid Theory and How It Grew." *American Music* 1, no. 2 (1983): 53–69.

Evans, James H., Jr. "Black Theology." In *A New Handbook of Christian Theology,* ed. Donald W. Musser and Joseph L. Price, 69–75. Nashville: Abingdon Press, 1992.

———. *We Have Been Believers: An African American Systematic Theology.* Minneapolis: Fortress Press, 1992.

Bibliography

Felder, Cain Hope. "Cultural Ideology, Afrocentrism and Biblical Interpretation." In *Black Theology: A Documentary History.* Vol. 2: *1980–1992,* ed. James H. Cone and Gayraud S. Wilmore, 184–95. 2nd ed. Maryknoll, N.Y.: Orbis Books, 1993.

Felder, Cain Hope, ed. *The Original African Heritage Study Bible.* Nashville: James C. Winston, 1993.

First Institutional Baptist Church. *AACTS Ministry: "To God Be the Glory."* Phoenix: New Day Video Productions, 1996. Videocassette.

———. *AACTS Parent-Student Handbook.* Phoenix: First Institutional Baptist Church, 1996.

———. "AACTS 1996–97 Pre K–6th Grade Program: Introducing the 'New' Middle School Program, 7th–9th Grades." First Institutional Baptist Church. Phoenix, 1996.

Fisher, Miles Mark. *Negro Slave Songs in the United States.* 1953. Reprint, New York: Carol Publishing Group, 1981.

Forde, Daryll, and G. I. Jones. *The Ibibio-Speaking Peoples of South-Eastern Nigeria.* London: Oxford University Press, 1950.

Franklin, John Hope. *From Slavery to Freedom: A History of Negro Americans.* 5th ed. New York: Alfred A. Knopf, 1980.

Frazier, E. Franklin. *The Negro Church in America.* New York: Schocken Books, 1963.

———. *The Negro in the United States.* Rev. ed. New York: Macmillan, 1957.

Gates, Louis Henry, and Nellie Y. McKay, eds. *The Norton Anthology of African American Literature.* New York: W. W. Norton, 1997.

Genovese, Eugene D. *Roll Jordan Roll: The World the Slaves Made.* New York: Pantheon Books, 1974.

Gilkes, Cheryl Townsend. "The Black Church as a Therapeutic Community: Suggested Areas for Research into the Black Religious Experience." *Journal of the Interdenominational Theological Center* 7, no. 1 (Fall 1980): 29–44.

———. "Womanist Ways of Seeing." In *Black Theology: A Documentary History.* Vol. 2: *1980–1992,* ed. James H. Cone and Gayraud S. Wilmore, 321–24. 2nd ed. Maryknoll, N.Y.: Orbis Books, 1993.

Grant, Jacquelyn. *White Women's Christ and Black Women's Jesus: Feminist Christology and Womanist Response.* Atlanta: Scholars Press, 1989.

Bibliography

———. "Womanist Jesus and the Mutual Struggle for Liberation." In *The Recovery of Black Presence: An Interdisciplinary Exploration,* ed. Randall C. Bailey and Jacquelyn Grant, 129–42. Nashville: Abingdon Press, 1995.

Grimes, Howard. "Theological Foundations for Christian Education." In *An Introduction to Christian Education,* ed. Marvin J. Taylor, 32–41. Nashville: Abingdon Press, 1966.

Habtu, Hailu. "The Fallacy of the 'Triple-Heritage' Thesis: A Critique." *Issue* 13 (1984): 26–29.

Hale, Janice E. "The Transmission of Faith to Young African American Children." In *The Recovery of Black Presence: An Interdisciplinary Exploration,* ed. Randall C. Bailey and Jacquelyn Grant, 193–207. Nashville: Abingdon Press, 1995.

Hamilton, Virginia, comp. *Her Stories: African American Folktales, Fairy Tales, and True Tales.* New York: The Blue Sky Press, 1995.

Hare, Maud Cuney. "The Source." In *The Negro in Music and Art,* ed. Lindsay Patterson, 19–30. International Library of Negro Life and History. 1935. Reprint, New York: Publishers Company, 1967.

Harris, James H. *Pastoral Theology: A Black-Church Perspective.* Minneapolis: Fortress Press, 1991.

Harris, Maria. *Fashion Me a People: Curriculum in the Church.* Louisville, Ky.: Westminster/John Knox Press, 1989.

———. *Teaching and Religious Imagination: An Essay in the Theology of Teaching.* New York: HarperCollins, 1987.

———. *Women and Teaching: Themes for a Spirituality of Pedagogy.* New York: Paulist Press, 1988.

Herskovits, Melville J. *The Myth of the Negro Past.* Boston: Beacon Press, 1958.

Higginson, Thomas Wentworth. "Slave Songs and Spirituals." In *Afro-American Religious History: A Documentary Witness,* ed. Milton C. Sernett, 110–32. Durham, N.C.: Duke University Press, 1985.

Hill, Paul, Jr. *Coming of Age: African American Male Rites of Passage.* Chicago: African American Images, 1992.

———. "Raising Male Children." *The Drum: National Rites of Passage Institute* 1, no. 2 (1994): 1–9.

Hill, Renee. "Who Are We for Each Other? Sexism, Sexuality and Womanist Theology." In *Black Theology: A Documentary History.* Vol. 2: *1980–1992,* ed. James H. Cone and Gayraud S. Wilmore, 345–51. 2nd ed. Maryknoll, N.Y.: Orbis Books, 1993.

Bibliography

Hine, Darlene Clark, Elsa Barkley Brown, and Rosalyn Terborg-Penn, eds. *Black Women in America: An Historical Encyclopedia.* Vols. 1 and 2. Bloomington: Indiana University Press, 1994.

Hopkins, Dwight N. "Slave Theology in the 'Invisible Institution.'" In *Cut Loose Your Stammering Tongue: Black Theology in the Slave Narratives,* ed. Dwight N. Hopkins and George Cummings, 1–45. Maryknoll, N.Y.: Orbis Books, 1991.

Hughes, Langston. "The Negro Speaks of Rivers." In *American Negro Poetry,* ed. Arna Bontemps, 63–64. New York: Hill and Wang, 1963.

Hurston, Zora Neale. "Spirituals and Neo-Spirituals." In *The Negro in Music and Art,* ed. Lindsay Patterson, 15–17. International Library of Negro Life and History, 1933. Reprint, New York: Publishers Company, 1967.

Hyman, Mark. *Blacks before America.* Trenton, N.J.: Africa World Press, 1994.

Idowu, E. Bolaji. *Olodumare: God in Yoruba Belief.* London: Longmans, Green and Co., 1962.

Jackson, Harold A., Jr. "The Negro Spiritual as Religious Expression and Historical Experience." *Journal of the Blaisdell Institute* 9, no. 1 (Fall and Winter 1973–74): 35–45.

———. "The New Hermeneutic and the Understanding of Spirituals." *Journal of the Interdenominational Theological Center* 33, no. 2 (Spring 1976): 36–48.

Jackson, Mahalia. "Joshua Fit the Battle of Jericho." *The Best of Mahalia Jackson.* New York: Sony Music Entertainment, Inc., 1995. Audiocassette.

Johnson, Charles, Patricia Smith, and the WGBH Series Research Team. *Africans in America: America's Journey through Slavery.* New York: Harcourt Brace, 1998.

Johnson, Clifton H., ed. *God Struck Me Dead: Voices of Ex-Slaves.* Cleveland: Pilgrim Press, 1969.

Johnson, Diane J., ed. *Proud Sisters: The Wisdom and Wit of African-American Women.* White Plains, N.Y.: Peter Pauper Press, 1995.

Johnson, James Weldon. "O Black and Unknown Bards." In *American Negro Poetry,* ed. Arna Bontemps, 1–2. New York: Hill and Wang, 1963.

Johnson, James Weldon, ed. *The Book of American Negro Spirituals.* New York: Viking Press, 1925.

Bibliography

Jones, Arthur C. *Wade in the Water: The Wisdom of the Spirituals.* Maryknoll, N.Y.: Orbis Books, 1993.

Jones, Bessie, and Bess Lomax Hawes. *Step It Down: Games, Plays, Songs, and Stories from the Afro-American Heritage.* Athens, Ga.: University of Georgia Press, 1972.

Jones, Thomas. "How I Learned to Read and Write." In *Steal Away: Stories of the Runaway Slaves,* compiled by Abraham Chapman, 73–80. New York: Praeger, 1971.

Keely, Barbara Anne. "Letty M. Russell: Educating for Partnership." In *Faith of Our Foremothers: Women Changing Religious Education,* ed. Barbara Anne Keely, 166–79. Louisville, Ky.: Westminster John Knox Press, 1997.

Kelly Miller Smith Institute, Inc. "What Does It Mean to Be Black and Christian?" In *Black Theology: A Documentary History.* Vol. 2: *1980–1992,* ed. James H. Cone and Gayraud S. Wilmore, 160–74. 2nd ed. Maryknoll, N.Y.: Orbis Books, 1993.

Kirk-Duggan, Cheryl A. *Exorcizing Evil: A Womanist Perspective on the Spirituals.* Maryknoll, N.Y.: Orbis Books, 1997.

Langstaff, John, ed. *Climbing Jacob's Ladder: Heroes of the Bible in African-American Spirituals.* New York: Margaret K. McElderry Books, 1991.

———. *What a Morning! The Christmas Story in Black Spirituals.* New York: Margaret K. McElderry Books, 1987.

Lemelle, Sid. *Pan-Africanism for Beginners.* New York: Writers and Readers Publishing, 1992.

Lester, Julius. *Black Folktales.* New York: Grove Press, 1969.

Levine, Lawrence W. *Black Culture and Black Consciousness: Afro-American Folk Thought from Slavery to Freedom.* New York: Oxford University Press, 1977.

Lincoln, C. Eric, and Lawrence H. Mamiya. *The Black Church in the African American Experience.* Durham, N.C.: Duke University Press, 1990.

Lovell, John, Jr. *Black Song: The Forge and the Flame.* New York: Macmillan, 1972.

Malson, Michelene R. *Understanding Black Single Parent Families: Stresses and Strengths.* Work in Progress, no. 25. Wellesley, Mass.: Stone Center for Developmental Services and Studies, 1987.

Mapson, J. Wendell, Jr. *The Ministry of Music in the Black Church.* Valley Forge, Pa.: Judson Press, 1984.

Bibliography

Martin, Clarice J. "Womanist Interpretations of the New Testament: The Quest for Holistic and Inclusive Translation and Interpretation." In *Black Theology: A Documentary History.* Vol. 2: *1980–1992,* ed. James H. Cone and Gayraud S. Wilmore, 225–44. 2nd ed. Maryknoll, N.Y.: Orbis Books, 1993.

Martin, Tony. *The Pan-African Connection: From Slavery to Garvey and Beyond.* Dover, Mass.: Majority Press, 1983.

Mazrui, Ali AlAmin. *The Africans: A Triple-Heritage.* Boston: Little, Brown, 1986.

Mbiti, John S. *African Religions and Philosophy.* New York: Frederick A. Praeger, 1969.

———. *Introduction to African Religion.* 2nd ed. 1975. Reprint, Oxford: Heinemann Educational Books, 1991.

McClain, William B. *Come Sunday: The Liturgy of Zion.* Nashville: Abingdon Press, 1990.

McNeill, Earldene, Judy Allen, Velma Schmidt, and Barbara McNeill Brierton, eds. *Cultural Awareness for Young Children.* Rev. ed. Dallas: The Learning Tree, 1981.

Mellon, James, ed. *Bullwhip Days: The Slaves Remember, An Oral History.* New York: Avon Books, 1988.

Miller, Randolph C. *The Clue to Christian Education.* New York: Charles Scribner's Sons, 1950.

Mitchell, Ella. "Oral Tradition: Legacy of Faith for the Black Church." *Religious Education* 81, no. 1 (Winter 1986): 93–112.

Mitchell, Henry H. *Black Belief: Folk Beliefs of Blacks in America and West Africa.* New York: Harper & Row, 1975.

Moore, Mary Elizabeth. "Rhythmic Curriculum: Guiding an Educative Journey." Paper presented in the symposium Les Rythmes Educatifs dans la Philosophie de Whitehead, Université Catholique de Lille, Lille, France, April 25–27, 1994. Handout.

Morrow, Delitha L. "Rites of Passage." *Upscale* (May 1993): 54–57.

Morton, Patricia. *Disfigured Images: The Historical Assault on Afro-American Women.* Westport, Conn.: Praeger, 1991.

Mulira, Jessie Gaston. "The Case of Voodoo in New Orleans." In *Africanisms in American Culture,* ed. Joseph E. Holloway, 34–68. Bloomington: Indiana University Press, 1990.

Nelson, C. Ellis. "The Curriculum of Christian Education." In *An Introduction to Christian Education,* ed. Marvin J. Taylor, 157–68. Nashville: Abingdon Press, 1966.

Bibliography

Newman, Richard. *Go Down, Moses: A Celebration of the African American Spiritual.* New York: Clarkson Potter, 1988.

Nichols, Paul. "Blacks and the Religious Education Movement." In *Changing Patterns of Religious Education,* ed. Marvin J. Taylor, 181–92. Nashville: Abingdon Press, 1984.

Odum, Howard W., and Guy B. Johnson. *The Negro and His Songs: A Study of Typical Negro Songs in the South.* Chapel Hill: University of North Carolina Press, 1925.

Ogbonnaya, A. Okechukwu. *On Communitarian Divinity: An African Interpretation of the Trinity.* New York: Paragon House, 1994.

Opoku, Kofi Asare. "Aspects of Akan Worship." In *The Black Experience in Religion,* ed. C. Eric Lincoln, 286–300. Garden City, N.Y.: Doubleday, Anchor Press, 1974.

Paris, Peter J. *The Spirituality of African Peoples: The Search for a Common Moral Discourse.* Minneapolis: Fortress Press, 1995.

Proctor, Henry Hugh. "The Theology of the Songs of the Southern Slave." *Journal of Black Sacred Music* 2, no. 1 (1988): 51–63.

Raboteau, Albert J. *Slave Religion: The "Invisible Institution" in the Antebellum South.* New York: Oxford University Press, 1978.

Radcliffe-Brown, A. R. Introduction to *African Systems of Kinship and Marriage,* ed. A. R. Radcliffe-Brown and Daryll Forde. New York: Oxford University Press, 1950.

Riggs, Marcia Y., ed. *Can I Get a Witness? Prophetic Religious Voices of African American Women: An Anthology.* Maryknoll, N.Y.: Orbis Books, 1997.

Roberts, J. Deotis. *Black Theology in Dialogue.* Philadelphia: Westminster Press, 1987.

Robinson, Aminah Brenda Lynn. *The Teachings: Drawn from African-American Spirituals.* San Diego: Harcourt Brace Jovanovich, 1992.

Rogers, Frank. "Dancing with Grace: Toward a Spirit-Centered Education." *School of Theology at Claremont, Occasional Paper* 1, no. 2 (1991).

Russell, Letty M. "Methodology in Liberation/Feminist Theologies: A Theological Spiral of Action/Reflection." 1994. Handout.

Russell, Letty M., ed. *Changing Contexts of Our Faith.* Philadelphia: Fortress Press, 1985.

Sanders, Cheryl J. "Afrocentric and Womanist Approaches to Theological Education." In *Living the Intersection: Womanism and Afrocentrism in Theology,* ed. Cheryl J. Sanders, 157–75. Minneapolis: Fortress Press, 1995.

Bibliography

Seymour, Jack, and Donald E. Miller. "Openings to God: Education and Theology in Dialogue." In *Theological Approaches to Christian Education*, ed. Jack Seymour and Donald E. Miller, 7–24. Nashville: Abingdon Press, 1990.

Shaw, Arnold. *Black Popular Music in America: From the Spirituals, Minstrels, and Ragtime to Soul, Disco, and Hip-Hop.* New York: Schirmer Books, 1986.

Shockley, Grant S. "Christian Education and the Black Church." In *Christian Education Journey of Black Americans: Past, Present, Future*, compiled by Charles Foster, Ethel R. Johnson, and Grant S. Shockley, 1–18. Nashville: Discipleship Resources, 1985.

———. "Liberation Theology, Black Theology, and Religious Education." In *Foundations for Christian Education in an Era of Change*, ed. Marvin J. Taylor, 80–95. Nashville: Abingdon Press, 1976.

Shorter, Aylward. *African Christian Theology: Adaptation or Incarnation?* Maryknoll, N.Y.: Orbis Books, 1977.

Smith, J. Alfred. Men's Day Sermon preached at Friendship Baptist Church, Yorba Linda, Calif., April 27, 1997.

Smith, Jessie Carney. *Notable Black Women.* Detroit: Gale Research, 1992.

Smith, William Farley. "Cries of Freedom in Afro-American Spirituals: Music/Worship Aids for Martin Luther King, Jr. Birthday Celebration and Black History Recognition." *Drew Gateway* 61, no. 1 (1991): 60–71.

———. *Songs of Deliverance: Organ Arrangements and Congregational Acts of Worship for the Church Year Based on African American Spirituals.* Nashville: Abingdon Press, 1996.

Smith, Yolanda Y. "Forming Wisdom through Cultural Rootedness." In *In Search of Wisdom: Faith Formation in the Black Church*, ed. Anne S. Wimberly and Evelyn L. Parker, 40–56. Nashville: Abingdon Press, 2002.

———. "He Still Wid Us — Jesus: The Musical Theology of the Spirituals." *Christian History* 18, no. 2 (1999): 18–19.

Songs of Zion. Nashville: Abingdon Press, 1981.

Southern, Eileen. *The Music of Black Americans: A History.* New York: W. W. Norton, 1971.

Spalding, Henry D., ed. *Encyclopedia of Black Folklore and Humor.* Middle Village, N.Y.: Jonathan David, 1972, 1990.

Spencer, Jon Michael. "Freedom Songs of the Civil Rights Movement." *Journal of Black Sacred Music* 1, no. 2 (1987): 1–16.

Bibliography

———. *Protest and Praise: Sacred Music of Black Religion.* Minneapolis: Fortress Press, 1990.

Stokes, Olivia Pearl. "Black Theology: A Challenge to Religious Education." In *Religious Education and Theology,* ed. Norma H. Thompson, 71–99. Birmingham, Ala.: Religious Education Press, 1982.

———. "The Educational Role of Black Churches in the 70s and 80s," 3–27. Philadelphia: United Church Press, Joint Educational Development, 1973. One of three monographs in the packet *New Roads to Faith.*

Stuckey, Sterling. *Slave Culture: Nationalist Theory and the Foundations of Black America.* New York: Oxford University Press, 1987.

Sweetman, David. *Women as Leaders in African History.* Portsmouth, N.H.: Heinemann Educational Books, 1984.

Talbot, Percy Amaury. *The Peoples of Southern Nigeria.* 3 vols. London: Oxford University Press, 1926.

Taylor, M. W. *Harriet Tubman.* New York: Chelsea House, 1991.

Terborg-Penn, Rosalyn, S. Harley, and A. B. Rushing, eds. *Women in Africa and the African Diaspora.* Washington, D.C.: Howard University Press, 1989.

Thurman, Howard. *Deep River and the Negro Spiritual Speaks of Life and Death.* 1975. Reprint, Richmond, Ind.: Friends United Press, 1990.

Tobin, Jacqueline L., and Raymond G. Dobard. *Hidden in Plain View: A Secret Story of Quilts and the Underground Railroad.* New York: Doubleday, 1999.

Walker, Alice. *In Search of Our Mothers' Gardens: Womanist Prose.* San Diego: Harcourt Brace, 1983.

Walker, Margaret. *This Is My Century: New and Collected Poems.* Athens: University of Georgia Press, 1989.

Walker, Wyatt Tee. *"Somebody's Calling My Name": Black Sacred Music and Social Change.* 1979. Reprint, Valley Forge, Pa.: Judson Press, 1990.

Walters, Ronald W. *Pan Africanism in the African Diaspora: An Analysis of Modern Afrocentric Political Movements.* Detroit: Wayne State University Press, 1993.

Warfield-Coppock, Nsenga. *Adolescent Rites of Passage.* Vol. 1 of *Afrocentric Theory and Applications.* Washington, D.C.: Baobab Associates, 1990.

———. *Images of African Sisterhood: Initiation and Rites of Passage to Womanhood.* Washington, D.C.: Baobab Associates, 1994.

Bibliography

Warren, Gwendolin Sims. *Ev'ry Time I Feel the Spirit: 101 Best-Loved Psalms, Gospel Hymns, and Spiritual Songs of the African-American Church*. New York: Henry Holt, 1997.

Washington, James M., ed. *A Testament of Hope: The Essential Writings and Speeches of Martin Luther King, Jr*. New York: HarperCollins, 1986.

Webber, Thomas L. *Deep Like the Rivers: Education in the Slave Quarter Community, 1831–1865*. New York: W. W. Norton, 1978.

Weems, Renita J. *Just a Sister Away: A Womanist Vision of Women's Relationships in the Bible*. San Diego: LuraMedia, 1988.

West, Cornel. *Race Matters*. Boston: Beacon Press, 1993.

Wiley, Christine Y. "A Ministry of Empowerment: A Holistic Model for Pastoral Counseling in the African American Community." *Journal of Pastoral Care* 45, no. 4 (Winter 1991): 355–65.

Wilkerson, Barbara, ed. *Multicultural Religious Education*. Birmingham, Ala.: Religious Education Press, 1997.

Williams, Delores. *Sisters in the Wilderness: The Challenge of Womanist God-Talk*. Maryknoll, N.Y.: Orbis Books, 1993.

Williams, Willard A. *Educational Ministries with Blacks*. Nashville: Board of Discipleship, United Methodist Church, 1974.

———. *Educational Ministry in the Black Community: Resource Booklet*. Nashville: Board of Education, United Methodist Church, 1972.

Wilmore, Gayraud S. *Black Religion and Black Radicalism: An Interpretation of the Religious History of Afro-American People*. 2nd ed. Maryknoll, N.Y.: Orbis Books, 1983.

Wilson, Amos N. *Black-on-Black Violence: The Psychodynamics of Black Self-Annihilation in Service of White Domination*. New York: Afrikan World Infosystems, 1990.

Wimberly, Anne S. *Soul Stories: African American Christian Education*. Nashville: Abingdon Press, 1994.

Wood, Frances E. "Take My Yoke Upon You." In *A Troubling in My Soul*, ed. Emilie M. Townes, 37–47. Maryknoll, N.Y.: Orbis Books, 1993.

Work, John W., ed. *American Negro Songs and Spirituals*. New York: Bonanza Books, 1940.

Wright, Jeremiah A., Jr. "Music as Cultural Expression in Black Church Theology and Worship." *Journal of Black Sacred Music* 3, no. 1 (1989): 1–5.

Yellin, Jean Fagan, ed. *Incidents in the Life of a Slave Girl: Written by Herself*. Cambridge, Mass.: Harvard University Press, 1987.

Young, Josiah U., III. "God's Path and Pan-Africa." In *Black Theology: A Documentary History.* Vol. 2: *1980–1992,* ed. James H. Cone and Gayraud S. Wilmore, 18–25. 2nd ed. Maryknoll, N.Y.: Orbis Books, 1993.

———. *A Pan-African Theology: Providence and the Legacies of the Ancestors.* Trenton, N.J.: Africa World Press, 1992.

Young, Richard, and Judy Dockrey Young. *African-American Folktales for Young Readers.* Little Rock: August House, 1993.

Index

AACTS. *See* African American Christian Training School
African American Christian heritage, church's central role in, 42–43
African American Christian Training School, 21–22, 145
African American Christian Worship (Costen), 46
African American church
  affirming biblical understanding of human freedom, 39
  movement of Holy Spirit in, 4
  need to explore new models of Christian education, 6
  reclaiming Christian themes in, 43–47
  role of, 42–43
  spirituals as source for enhancing educational ministry, 77–78
  subjugation of women, role in, 92
  theology and Christian education related in, 84
African American culture, heroes and heroines, 32–36
African American heritage, 29–36
African American religion, link to African religion, 65–66
African Americans
  assault on self-esteem of, 23–26
  celebrating heritage, 36
  common experience of, 30–32
  hopelessness among, 12
  little knowledge of heritage, 30
  unique elements of Christian heritage, 36–43

"African Canticle, An" (African prayer), 124–25
African culture
  devalued, 23–25
  history, negative portrayal of, 26
  music, 1–2, 69
  standards of beauty rejected, 25–26
African heritage, 22–29
Africanness, rejection of, 22–23
Africans
  cosmology of, 63
  influence on spirituals, 65–69
  musical tradition, 64–65
  worldview, 62–64
  Western culture's impact on, 11
African spirit songs, paganism of, 57
Africans, The: A Triple-Heritage (Mazrui), 49n1
African traditional religion, 64, 80n37
Afrocentrism, 26, 28–29, 94–95
Allen, William Francis, 69–70, 127
Amistad, 132
Angelou, Maya, 139
antiphonal reading, 141n4
antiphony, 60
Asante, Molefi Kete, 28–29, 49n1, 94
Awolalu, J. Omosade, 80n37

Baker-Fletcher, Karen, 90
Bantu, 68
baptism, 137–38
Barrett, Leonard, 26
Bible, role in womanist theology, 92–93

Index

biblical interpretation, shaped by dominant culture, 10–11
biblicism, in spirituals, 58–59
Birthing Project, 46–47
Black-on-Black Violence (Wilson), 11–12
Black History Month, 150–51
blackness
  of Christ, 87
  negative understanding of, 25–26
black power movement, 85
black theology, 84–86
  central claims, 87
  Christian education and, 88–89
  inaccessibility of, 97
  sources of, 87
Bontemps, Arna, 33
Bornou people, 68
Brer Rabbit, 33–34
Burlin, Natalie Curtis, 123

call-and-response, 17, 40, 60, 68, 116–17
choral reading, 118, 141n4
Christ. *See also* Jesus
  blackness of, 87
  working toward liberation of black women, 92
Christian education. *See also* Christian education, triple-heritage model of
  African American church's need to explore new models of, 6
  African American churches distancing from triple-heritage, 5, 10
  beginning with Spirit of God, 5
  black theology and, 88–89
  contextualizing, 94, 95
  effective methods from African American perspective, 77–78
  holistic approach to, 48
  related to theology, 83–84
  Spirit-centered model of, 113–14
  womanist theology and, 93–95
Christian education, triple-heritage model of
  African American component, 30
  African component, 29
  characteristics of, 17–20
  Christian component, 36
  collaborative nature, 13–14
  creative methodology, 147
  creative process of, 18
  creative programming, 148–49
  criterion for, 16
  curriculum for, 15–16, 149
  defining, 12–20
  dialogue encouraged, 17
  effects of grounding in, 12
  encouraging cooperation, 19–20
  encouraging critical reflection, 18–19
  fun approach to, 150–52
  insights from black and womanist theology, 95–97
  insights from spirituals, 111–14
  nurture, 146–47
  pastoral leadership for, 144–45
  purpose of, 14–15
  starting point for, 16
  teacher training, 145–46
Christian ethics, slaves' beliefs about, 111
Christian heritage, distinctive elements for African Americans, 37–43
Christianity, influence on spirituals, 2
Christian Studies Institute, 148
Christian themes, reclaiming in African American church, 43–47
church
  central role in African American Christian heritage, 42
  challenged to provide holistic educational ministry, 48
  declining influence on African Americans, 43–44
  present needs of, 4–5, 18, 32

Index

civil rights movement, 59–60, 84
closing ritual, 139
coded meanings. *See* hidden meanings
coding, 66–67
collage, 132
communal approach, 17
communal remembering, 112
community
   African understanding of, 23–24
   balance with individual, 24
   basis of African worldview, 63–64
   creating educational programs for, 152
   music sung in and for, 69
   prayer in, 41
   service toward, 46–47
   spirituals inspiring sense of, 113
Cone, James, 57, 85, 87, 108
conjure, 108
connectedness, 63
contemporary heroes/heroines, 35–36
cosmos, 65–66
Costen, Melva, 44, 46, 105, 113–14
creation, study of, 134
Creel, Margaret, 64
Crockett, Joseph, 77–78
cultural concerns, worship addressing, 40
cultural sensitivity, 48
curriculum design, 15–16, 149

Deep River and the Negro Spiritual Speaks of Life and Death (Thurman), 73–74
dialogue, 116–20
directed action, 47
discipleship model of training, 146
double meaning. *See* hidden meanings
dramatic presentation, 121–22
drums, 126–27
Du Bois, W. E. B., 41, 55, 57

education
   African American church's role in, 43
   artistic approach to, 120–21
   cultural sources for, 48
   praxis approach to, 48
educational model, theoretical and operational, 88–89
educational program design, 77
eschatology, slaves' beliefs about, 109–11
Eurocentrism, 10–11, 94
evil, slaves' beliefs about, 108–9

faith, church's role in shaping, 43–44
faith conversion, Spirit's role in, 105
fashioning, 14
Fashion Me a People (Harris), 14
Felder, Cain Hope, 10–11
fictional heroes/heroines, 33–34
First Institutional Baptist Church (Phoenix), 144–45, 146, 148, 150
Fisher, Miles Mark, 126
Fisk University Jubilee Singers, 70
five-part meditation, 129–30
"For My People" (Walker), 119–20
Forten, Charlotte, 69
Frazier, E. Franklin, 51n19
freedom, shifting meaning of, 39
freedom songs, 18, 19
the frenzy, 41

Garrison, Lucy McKim, 69–70, 127
God
   African American church view of, 39
   African understanding of, 23
   personal knowledge of, 44
   renewed faith in, 44–45
   in slaves' religion, 3, 66, 102–3
   in womanist theology, 91
Goncalvez, Antam, 27

Index

Grant, Jacquelyn, 91–92
Green, Jackie L., 21
group learning, 10

Habtu, Hailu, 49n1
Hamer, Fannie Lou, 18
Hare, Maud Cuney, 56–57
Harris, James H., 44, 45
Harris, Maria, 14, 112, 120–21
heaven, slaves' beliefs about, 109
hell, slaves' beliefs about, 109–10
heroes/heroines, 32–36
Herskovits, Melville, 26
hidden meanings, 2, 18, 60, 70, 110, 130
Higginson, Thomas Wentworth, 69
High John de Conqueror, 34
history, importance of, 47
holy boldness, 41
Holy Spirit
   movement in African American church, 4
   presence in worship in African American church, 41
   role in church's educational ministry, 5
   slaves' beliefs about, 104–6
Hopkins, Dwight, 108
"How I Learned to Read and Write" (Jones), 125
Hughes, Langston, 135
humanity, slaves' beliefs about, 106–8
Hurston, Zora Neale, 18, 56, 57

imagery, 61, 120–22
imagination, 120–22
improvisation, 18, 19, 59–60
individualism, effect on African American family, 24
invisible institution, 37–38, 70, 106, 113
iron kettles, role in worship services, 70–71

Jesus. *See also* Christ
   acknowledging liberating activity of, 44
   African American view of, 39
   birth of as theme in spirituals, 75
   historical context of, 87
   message of, 44–45
   parables of, 134–35
   restoring confidence in liberating work of, 85–86
   slaves' beliefs about, 103–4
   in womanist theology, 91–92
Johnson, James Weldon, 118–19
Jones, Arthur C., 57
Jones, Thomas, 125

kinship, 46

leadership, model of, 89
learning
   cognitive model of, 89
   holistic model of, 89
Lee, Jarena, 91–92
Lemelle, Sid, 27
Levine, Lawrence, 33, 34, 117
liberation legacy, 30–32
life, affirmation of, 63
Lincoln, C. Eric, 39
litany, 141n4
Living the Intersection: Womanism and Afrocentrism in Theology (Sanders, ed.), 94
love, reaffirming, 45–46
love ethic, 45

Mamiya, Lawrence M., 39
Mazrui, Ali AlAmin, 49n1
Mbiti, John, 133, 136
message, eternality of, in spirituals, 59
metaphor, 133–34
methodology, for building triple-heritage model of Christian education, 147

Index

Mitchell, Ella, 16
Mitchell, Henry, 22–23
Moore, Mary Elizabeth, 15
Mulira, Jessie, 64
music
   accompaniment to ritual observances, 137
   in African American church, 40
   in African life, 64–65
musical/speech choir, 119–20

narrative, 130–32
Narrative of Travels in Northern and Central Africa (Denham and Clapperton), 68
National Committee of Black Churchmen, 86
nature, 132–36
nature walk, 136
"Negro Speaks of Rivers, The" (Hughes), 135
Neo-Spirituals, 56
New Testament, resource for spirituals, 74
Nichols, Paul, 84
nurture, 146–47

object lessons, 133–34
"O Black and Unknown Bards" (Johnson), 118–19
Ogbonnaya, A. Okechukwu, 24, 63
Old Testament, influence on spirituals, 57, 74
opening ritual, 139
oppression
   effect on interpretation of humanity and freedom, 39
   effect on theology, 38–39
oral tradition, 15, 38, 131
otherworldliness, 107–8

Pan-Africanism, 26, 27–28, 29
pantomime, 125–26

pastoral leadership, 144–45
Pastoral Theology: A Black-Church Perspective (Harris), 45
pedagogy, African-centered, 10
poetry, 135
politics of conversion, 45
praise, 41
praise songs, 112
prayer, 15, 40–41
preaching, 40
Proctor, Henry H., 102, 111
programming, for building triple-heritage model of Christian education, 148–49
protests, 32
Psalms, using to study rhythm in Bible, 128

racism
   effect on interpretation of humanity and freedom, 39
   effect on theology, 38–39
Reagon, Bernice Johnson, 18
relatedness, 46
religion, central to Africans' being, 64
religious experiences, influence on spirituals, 75–76
religious resistance, 32
repetition, 61, 68
resistance, 31–32, 76
responsive reading, 141n4
resurrection
   slaves' beliefs about, 110
   theme in spirituals, 74
rhythm, 59, 126–30
ring shout, 127–28
ritual, 136–41
ritual of remembrance, 139–40

sacredness, 63, 110
Sanders, Cheryl, 91, 94–95
Satan, slaves' beliefs about, 108–9
service, returning, 46

Index

sin, slaves' beliefs about, 108–9
slave heroes/heroines, 34–35
slave religion, 37–38, 73–76
slavery
   context for African American Christianity, 37
   devaluing of African culture during, 23
   influence on spirituals, 2
   resistance to, 24–25, 31–32
slaves
   conveying religious beliefs, 65–66
   private worship services, 70
   understanding of God, 3
Smith, J. Alfred, 36
Smith, William Farley, 137
socialization, model of, 89
Somebody's Calling My Name (Walker), 58–62
song titles. *See* spirituals, titles
sorrow songs, 55–56
Spirit-centered education, 5, 113–14
spirituals. *See also* spirituals, titles
   African musical characteristics reflected in, 68
   African roots, 62–69
   alternative names for, 79n14
   characteristics of, 58–62
   coding used in, 66–67
   collecting, 69–70
   creation of slave community, 19
   development of, 69–73
   drawing together elements of triple-heritage, 13–14
   dual purposes of, 73
   educational qualities of, 116
   embodying triple-heritage, 4
   function in slaves' work environment, 71
   as historical songs, 57–58
   influence on other music, 73
   influence on wider society, 78

spirituals (*continued*)
   insights for triple-heritage model of Christian education, 111–14
   learning, 15
   meant for singing with a group, 56, 58
   nature of, 55–58
   Old Testament influence on, 57, 174
   popularity of, 70
   in process of creation, 18, 56
   reflecting encounter with Christianity, 73–76
   religion highly regarded, 67
   role in slaves' worship services, 71
   as sorrow songs, 55–56
   source for enhancing educational ministry, 77–78
   sources of, 73–74
   themes and functions, 58
   theology of, 4–5, 102–14
   used to express hope and despair, 72–73
   used as form of social critique, 4
   use in triple-heritage model of Christian education, 1–2, 152–54
   worldview of, 62–64
spirituals, titles
   "Ain't Dat Good News"? 126
   "All God's Chillun Got Wings," 110
   "Balm in Gilead," 106
   "Calvary," 74, 104, 121–22
   "Captain, O Captain," 72
   "Certainly, Lord," 75–76, 126
   "Come, Sinner, Come," 109
   "Deep River," 132, 135
   "Didn't It Rain?" 130
   "Didn't My Lord Deliver Daniel?" 74, 103, 130
   "Done Made My Vow to the Lord," 120
   "Don' Let Nobody Turn You Aroun'," 18, 59–60
   "Ev'ry Time I Feel the Spirit," 128

spirituals, titles (*continued*)
   "Ezek'el Saw de Wheel," 57, 130
   "Glory, Glory, Hallelujah," 129
   "Go, Tell It on the Mountain," 75, 130
   "God Is a God," 59, 134
   "Go Down, Moses," 60, 74, 130–31
   "He Arose," 104
   "He Never Said a Mumbalin' Word," 74
   "He's Got the Whole World in His Hands," 66, 133–34
   "Hush, Hush, Somebody's Callin' Mah Name," 61
   "I'll Be Alright," 73
   "I'm Gonna Sing," 124, 128
   "I've Been 'Buked," 126
   "John Henry," 71–72
   "Joshua Fit de Battle of Jericho," 59, 129, 130
   "Keep a-Inchin' Along," 75, 133
   "Kum Ba Yah, My Lord," 117
   "Lit'l Boy, How Ole Are You?" 75
   "Little David, Play on Your Harp," 130
   "Lord, I Want to Be a Christian," 117
   "Mary Had a Baby," 75
   "O Freedom," 76, 107
   "Oh, Wasn't Dat a Wide Ribber," 68–69
   "Raise the Iron," 72
   "Ride On, King Jesus," 103–4
   "Sister Mary Had-a But One Child," 75
   "Somebody's Knocking at Your Door," 120
   "Sometimes I Feel Like a Motherless Chile," 126
   "Steal Away," 2–3, 60
   "Swing Low, Sweet Chariot," 60, 120
   "This Little Light of Mine," 59, 139

spirituals, titles (*continued*)
   "Three Wise Men to Jerusalem Came," 75
   "Wade in the Water," 137–38
   "Wake Up, Jonah!" 130
   "Were You There?" 61, 74
   "We Shall Overcome," 73, 120
   "Woke Up This Morning with My Mind Stayed on Freedom," 73
Spirituals and the Blues, The (Cone), 57
spontaneity, 122–26
spontaneous readings, 124–25
Stewart, Warren H., Sr., 21
Stokes, Olivia Pearl, 42, 84
story, as mode of education, 131–32
story-linking, 49
storytelling, 38, 40, 132
survival legacy, 30–32

teacher training, 145–46
theology. *See also* black theology, womanist theology
   African American Christian approach, 38–39
   oppression and racism's effect on, 38–39
   reinterpretation of, affirmed for black experience, 86
   related to Christian education, 83–84
   of spirituals, 102–14
Thurman, Howard, 73–74, 76, 103, 104, 107, 132
trickster, 33–34
triple-heritage
   African American Christian Training School view of, 21–22
   African heritage, 22–29
   effects of grounding Christian education in, 12
   holistic view, 21–22

Index

triple-heritage (*continued*)
   insights from black and womanist theology, 95–97
   insights from spirituals for model of Christian education, 111–14
   insights for teaching, 47–49
   intertwining aspects of, 3–4, 12–14
   purpose of teaching, 1
   river as metaphor for, 3–4
   spirituals encouraging pride in, 113
   using spirituals to teach, 1–2, 116
Truth, Sojourner, 91–92
Tubman, Harriet, 2, 19
tuning, 41
Turner, Nat, 2–3

Underground Railroad, 2, 19

Walker, Alice, 90
Walker, Margaret, 119–20
Walker, Wyatt T., 58–62
Ware, Charles Pickard, 69–70, 127
West, Cornel, 45
Williams, Delores, 25, 91
Williams, Willard, 86
Wilmore, Gayraud, 24–25
Wilson, Amos, 11–12
Wimberly, Anne, 49
womanist theology, 89–92
   Christian education and, 93–95
   inaccessibility of, 97
work songs, 71–72
worship
   African American Christian approach, 40–41
   Spirit's role in, 105–6
worship services, during slavery, 38

Yale Black Seminarians, 119–20